THE BEST OF
ANDREW MURRAY

THE BEST OF
ANDREW MURRAY

BAKER BOOK HOUSE
Grand Rapids, Michigan

Copyright 1952 by
Fleming H. Revell Company

Reprinted November, 1978 by
Baker Book House Company
with permission of copyright owner

Formerly published under the title:
The Treasury of Andrew Murray

ISBN: 0-8010-6069-9

First printing, November 1978
Second printing, September 1979

PHOTOLITHOPRINTED BY CUSHING - MALLOY, INC.
ANN ARBOR, MICHIGAN, UNITED STATES OF AMERICA
1979

Contents

Introduction   7

The Power of United Prayer   13
from With Christ in the School of Prayer

The Power of Persevering Prayer   19
from With Christ in the School of Prayer

Prayer in Harmony with God   25
from With Christ in the School of Prayer

Like Christ: In His Dependence on the Father   31
from Like Christ

Like Christ: In His Love   37
from Like Christ

Like Christ: In His Praying   43
from Like Christ

Like Christ: In His Use of Scripture   49
from Like Christ

Like Christ: In Forgiving   55
from Like Christ

Abide in Christ, All Ye Who Have Come to Him   61
from Abide in Christ

Abide in Christ, Trusting Him to Keep You   67
from Abide in Christ

Abide in Christ and in His Love   73
from Abide in Christ

Christ Our Life   79
from The Master's Indwelling

Holiness and Happiness   91
From Holy in Christ

The Ministry of the Spirit   99
from The Spirit of Christ

The Spirit and the Flesh   107
from The Spirit of Christ

The Spirit Through Faith   115
    from The Spirit of Christ

How It Is to Be Found by All   121
    from The Full Blessing of Pentecost

In the Name of Christ   131
    from The Ministry of Intercession

Paul, a Pattern of Prayer   141
    from The Ministry of Intercession

On Learning Obedience   151
    from The School of Obedience

In Christian Experience   161
    from The Two Covenants

The Everlasting Covenant   167
    from The Two Covenants

Jesus the Mediator   175
    from The Two Covenants

The Humility of Jesus   183
    from Humility

The Presence of Christ   189
    from The Deeper Christian Life

Meditation   201
    from The Inner Chamber and the Inner Life

Waiting and Working   207
    from Working for God

Good Works, the Light of the World   211
    from Working for God

Christ's Estimate of Money   215
    from Thoughts for God's Stewards

The Holy Spirit and Money   223
    from Thoughts for God's Stewards

God Is Love   231
    from Love Made Perfect

Our Lord's Prayer   243
    from Love Made Perfect

Introduction

IN THE LIFE and work of Andrew Murray (1828-1917) God gave an unusual gift to the Church universal. Born of Scottish parents in South Africa, he was given a general education in Scotland for seven years, including the M.A. degree course at Aberdeen University. Then followed three years study of theology in Holland.

During the period in Scotland he was influenced by the scholarly preaching of evangelical Presbyterian ministers, including Chalmers, Candlish, McCheyne, and the two Bonars. The spiritual awakening of 1838-40 was similar to that which stirred America under Finney, and in the Rev. William C. Burns God found a man to use to a remarkable degree. His life profoundly moved young Andrew in the direction of revival and holiness of life.

Returning to the land of his boyhood, Andrew Murray spent the rest of his life as a minister of the Dutch Reformed Church. From that center of pastoral activity he reached countless thousands beyond his parish. This was done by conferences in America, Canada, and in Great Britain, and particularly by his published works. He early became the spiritual leader and teacher for the deepening of the Christian life. A household name in evangelical circles of another generation, it is a cause for thanksgiving that a selection of his writings now will introduce his message to a new constituency of readers.

Of this mentor of the spiritual life we can say in our Scotch vernacular that he was "far ben wi' the Master." His life was lived in the secret place, on intimate terms with the Most High. When he preached he came forth from the Presence and his writings distilled "the beaten oil of the sanctuary." He gave to the Church about 250 books and pamphlets in Dutch and English. A voluminous writer, he was also the flaming evangelist, the organizer of educational institutions, the devoted pastor, and the missionary statesman.

Reading this anthology and thesaurus is to be transported into a rarified atmosphere of spiritual light and life. The secret of our author is a sane mysticism, an inner life of the spirit out of which is the radiance of Christlike character and influence. These extracts can be classified as follows: (1) Prayer; (2) Holiness; and (3) Power.

The emphasis on PRAYER leads into the oratory of the soul and the still hour where we find our Lord as the supreme example and are taught to follow His steps. The ministry of intercession, the inner chamber, the sin of prayerlessness are dealt with by a wise physician of the soul.

When HOLINESS is the theme there is the stress on humility, beauty of character, the interior life, absolute surrender, learning to obey God's will, and likeness to Christ.

That the Church needed POWER was reiterated in the call for the continuous nature of Pentecost. Here is the divine indwelling, the power of the Holy Spirit, the full blessing, abiding in Christ, and our Lord's estimate of money and its use by God's stewards.

The teaching of this mystic of common-sense living was far-reaching in its reviving and upbuilding of the Church, its recruiting of men for service, and its thrust in the missionary enterprise. As he unfolded the intricacies of the heart, the man of God exemplified that abiding in Christ led to the abounding life of the Spirit. Here was experimental religion at white heat. Those who hungered were fed and all Christly lives were joined in a universal fellowship.

In this volume the style is terse and simple. The sentences stab and probe. This guide to richer life sends you back to the Bible text in every exposition. Here is his chief contribution. *You realize there is more in the Christian life than you have yet experienced.* Those who will follow him step by step, taking a little at a time, meditating and praying over it, will be amply rewarded. The teaching of this book—more than any other—can be a major factor in the revival of the Church today.

"Happy man," wrote Alexander Whyte to Andrew Murray, "you have been chosen and ordained of God *to go to the heart of things.*" To all who desire to share that rich heritage we commend this volume. It is our prayer and confident belief that God will again honor and bless the mission and ministry of Andrew Murray, the saint of South Africa.

RALPH G. TURNBULL

The Power
of United Prayer

Again I say unto you, That if two of you shall agree on earth as touching any thing that they shall ask, it shall be done for them of my Father which is in heaven. For where two or three are gathered together in my name, there am I in the midst of them.
MATTHEW 18: 19, 20.

ONE of the first lessons of our Lord in His school of prayer was: Not to be seen of men. Enter thy inner chamber; be alone with the Father. When He has thus taught us that the meaning of prayer is personal, individual contact with God, He comes with a second lesson: You have need not only of secret, solitary, but also of public, united prayer. And He gives us a very special promise for the united prayer of two or three who agree in what they ask. As a tree has its roots hidden in the ground and its stem growing up into the sunlight, so prayer needs equally for its full development the hidden secrecy in which the soul meets God alone, and the public fellowship with those who find in the name of Jesus their common meeting place.

The reason why this must be so is plain. The bond that unites a man to his fellow men is no less real and close than that which unites him to God; he is one with them. Grace renews not alone our relation to God but to man too. We not only learn to say "My Father," but "Our Father." Nothing would be more unnatural than that the children of a family should always meet their father separately, but never in the united expression of their desires or their love. Believers are not only members of one family, but even of one body. Just as each member of the body depends on the other, and the full action of the spirit dwelling in the body

13

depends on the union and co-operation of all, so Christians cannot reach the full blessing God is ready to bestow through His Spirit but as they seek and receive it in fellowship with each other. It is in the union and fellowship of believers that the Spirit can manifest His full power. It was to the hundred and twenty continuing in one place together, and praying with one accord, that the Spirit came from the throne of the glorified Lord.

The marks of true united prayer are given us in these words of our Lord. The first is *agreement* as to the thing asked. There must not only be generally the consent to agree with anything another may ask, there must be some special thing, some matter of distinct united desire; the agreement must be, as all prayer must be, in spirit and in truth. In such agreement it will become very clear to us what exactly we are asking, whether we may confidently ask according to God's will, and whether we are ready to believe that we have received what we ask.

The second mark is the gathering in, or into, the Name of Jesus. Afterwards we shall have much more to learn of the need and the power of the Name of Jesus in prayer; here our Lord teaches us that the Name must be the center of union to which believers gather, the bond of union that makes them one, just as a home contains and unites all who are in it. "The name of the Lord is a strong tower; the righteous runneth into it and escape." That Name is such a reality to those who understand and believe it, that to meet within it is to have Himself present. The love and unity of His disciples have infinite attraction for Jesus: "Where two or three are gathered in my name, *there am I in the midst of them.*" It is the living presence of Jesus, in the fellowship of His loving praying disciples, that gives united prayer its power.

The third mark is, the sure answer: "It shall be done for them of my Father." A prayer meeting for maintaining religious fellowship, or seeking our own edification, may have its use; this was not the Saviour's view in its appointment. He meant it as a means of securing *special answer to prayer.* A prayer meeting without recognized answer to prayer ought to be an anomaly. When any of us have distinct desires in regard to which we feel too weak to exercise the needful faith, we ought to seek strength in the help of others. In the unity of faith and of love and of the Spirit the power of the Name and the Presence of Jesus acts more freely and the answer comes more surely. The mark that there has been true united prayer is the fruit, the answer, the receiving of the thing we have asked: "I say unto you, *It shall be done* for them of my Father which is in heaven."

What an unspeakable privilege of united prayer this is, and what a power it might be. If the believing husband and wife knew that they were joined together in the Name of Jesus to experience His presence and power in united prayer (1 Peter); if friends believed what mighty help two or three praying in concert could give each other; if in every prayer meeting the coming together in the Name, the faith in the Presence, and the expectation of the answer, stood in the foreground; if in every church united effectual prayer were regarded as one of the chief purposes for which they are banded together, the highest exercise of their power as a church; if in the Church Universal the coming of the kingdom, the coming of the King Himself, first in the mighty outpouring of His Holy Spirit, then in His own glorious person, were really matter of unceasing united crying to God—Oh, who can say what blessing might come to, and through, those who thus agreed to prove God in the fulfilment of His promise.

In the Apostle Paul we see very distinctly what a reality his faith in the power of united prayer was. To the Romans he writes (15: 30): "I beseech you, brethren, by the love of the Spirit, that ye *strive together with me* in your prayers to God for me." He expects in answer to be delivered from his enemies, and to be prospered in his work. To the Corinthians (II Cor. 1: 10, 11), "God will still deliver us, ye also helping together on our behalf by your supplications," their prayer is to have a real share in his deliverance. To the Ephesians he writes: "With all prayer and supplication praying at all seasons in the Spirit for all the saints and on my behalf, that utterance may be given unto me." His power and success in his ministry he makes to depend on their prayers. With the Philippians (1: 19) he expects that his trials will turn to his salvation and the progress of the gospel *"through your supplications and* the supply of the Spirit of Jesus Christ." To the Colossians (4: 3) he adds to the injunction to continue steadfast in prayer, "withal praying for us also, that God may open unto us a door for the word." And to the Thessalonians (II Thess. 3: 1, 2) he writes: "Finally, brethren, pray for us, that the word of the Lord may run and be glorified, and that we may be delivered from unreasonable men." It is everywhere evident that Paul felt himself the member of a body, on the sympathy and co-operation of which he was dependent, and that he counted on the prayers of these churches to gain for him what otherwise might not be given. The prayers of the Church were to him as real a factor in the work of the kingdom as the power of God.

Who can say what power a church could develop and exercise if it gave itself to the work of prayer day and night for the coming of the kingdom, for God's power on His servants and His word, for the glorifying of God in the salvation of souls? Most churches think their members are gathered into one simply to take care of and build up each other. They know not that God rules the world by the prayers of His saints, that prayer is the power by which Satan is conquered, that by prayer the Church on earth has disposal of the powers of the heavenly world. They do not remember that Jesus has, by His promise, consecrated every assembly in His Name to be a gate of heaven, where His Presence is to be felt, and His Power experienced in the Father fulfilling their desires.

We cannot sufficiently thank God for the blessed week of united prayer with which Christendom in our days opens every year. As proof of our unity and our faith in the power of united prayer, as a training school for the enlargement of our hearts to take in all the needs of the Church Universal, as a help to united persevering prayer, it is of unspeakable value. But very specially as a stimulus to continued union in prayer in the smaller circles its blessing has been great. And it will become even greater, as God's people recognize what it is, all to meet as one in the Name of Jesus, to have His Presence in the midst of a body all united in the Holy Spirit, and boldly to claim the promise that it shall be done of the Father what they agree to ask.

Let us learn to give God time. God needs time with us . . . that is, time in the daily fellowship with Himself, for Him to exercise the full influence of His presence on us, and time, day by day, in the course of our being kept waiting, for faith to prove its reality and to fill our whole being. . . . Let no delay shake our faith.

The Power
of Persevering Prayer

*And he spake a parable unto them to the end that they ought
always to pray, and not to faint. . . . And the Lord said, Hear
what the unrighteous judge saith. And shall not God avenge
his own elect, which cry to him day and night, and yet he is
long-suffering over them? I say unto you, that he will avenge
them speedily.*

LUKE 18: 1-8.

OF ALL the mysteries of the prayer world the need of persevering prayer is one of the greatest. That the Lord, who is so loving and longing to bless, should have to be supplicated time after time, sometimes year after year, before the answer comes, we cannot easily understand. It is also one of the greatest practical difficulties in the exercise of believing prayer. When, after persevering supplication, our prayer remains unanswered, it is often easiest for our slothful flesh, and it has all the appearance of pious submission, to think that we must now cease praying, because God may have His secret reason for withholding His answer to our request.

It is by faith alone that the difficulty is overcome. When once faith has taken its stand on God's word and the Name of Jesus, and has yielded itself to the leading of the Spirit to seek God's will and honor alone in its prayer, it need not be discouraged by delay. It knows from Scripture that the power of believing prayer is simply irresistible; real faith can never be disappointed. It knows that just as water, to exercise the irresistible power it can have, must be gathered up and accumulated until the stream can come down in full force, so there must often be a heaping up of prayer until God sees that the measure is full, when the answer comes. It knows that just as the plowman has to take his ten thousand steps to sow his tens of thousand seeds, each one a part of the preparation for the final harvest, so there is a need for oft-repeated persevering prayer, all working out some desired blessing. It knows for certain that not a single believing prayer can fail of its effect in heaven, but has its influence, and is treasured up to work out an answer in due time to him who perseveres to the end. It knows that it has to do, not with human thoughts or possibilities, but with the word of the living God. And so, even as Abraham through so many years "in hope believed against hope," and then "through faith *and patience* inherited the promise," faith knows that the long-suffering of the Lord is salvation, *waiting* and *hasting* unto the coming of its Lord to fulfill His promise.

To enable us, when the answer to our prayer does not come at once, to combine quiet patience and joyful confidence in our persevering prayer, we must especially try to understand the two words in which our Lord sets forth the character and conduct, not of the unjust judge, but of our God and Father, toward those whom He allows to cry day and night to Him: "He is *long-suffering* over them; he will avenge them *speedily.*"

He will avenge them *speedily,* the Master says. The blessing is all prepared; He is not only willing, but most anxious, to give them what they ask; everlasting love burns with the longing desire to reveal itself fully to its beloved and to satisfy their needs. God will not delay one moment longer than is absolutely necessary; He will do all in His power to hasten and speed the answer.

But why, if this be true and His power be infinite, does it often require so long for the answer to prayer to come? And why must God's own elect so often, in the midst of suffering and conflict, cry day and night? "He is *long-suffering* over them." "Behold, the husbandman waiteth for the precious fruit of the earth, being patient over it, until it receive the early and the latter rain." The husbandman does, indeed, long for his harvest, but knows that it must have its full time of sunshine and rain, and he has long patience. A child so often wants to pick the half-ripe fruit; the husbandman knows how to wait till the proper time. Man, in his spiritual nature too, is under the law of gradual growth that reigns in all created life. It is only in the path of development that he can reach his divine destiny. And it is the Father, in whose hands are the times and seasons, who knows the moment when the soul or the Church is ripened to that fulness of faith in which it can really take and keep the blessing. As a father who longs to have his only child home from school, and yet waits patiently till the time of training is completed, so it is with God and His children: He is the long-suffering One, and answers speedily.

The insight into this truth leads the believer to cultivate the corresponding dispositions: *patience* and *faith, waiting* and *hasting,* are the secret of his perseverance. By faith in the promise of God, we know that we *have* the petitions we have asked of Him. Faith takes and holds the answer in the promise as an unseen spiritual possession, rejoices in it, and praises for it. But there is a difference between the faith that thus holds the word and knows that it has the answer and the clearer, fuller, riper faith that obtains the promise as a present experience. It is in persevering, not unbelieving, but confident and praising prayer, that the soul grows up into that full union with its Lord in which it can enter upon the possession of the blessing in Him. There may be in these around us, there may be in that great system of being of which we are part, there may be in God's government, things that have to be put right through our prayer ere the answer can fully come: the faith that has, according to the command, believed that it has received, can allow God to take His time; it knows it has prevailed and must prevail. In quiet, persistent, and determined perseverance it continues in prayer and thanksgiving until the blessing come. And so we see combined what at first sight appears so contradictory—the faith that rejoices in the answer of the unseen God as a present possession and the patience that cries day and night until it be revealed. The *speedily* of God's *long-suffering* is met by the triumphant but patient faith of His waiting child.

Our great danger, in this school of the answer delayed, is the temptation to think that, after all, it may not be God's will to give us what we ask. If our prayer be according to God's word, and under the leading of the Spirit, let us not give way to these fears. Let us learn to give God time. God needs time with us. If only we give Him time, that is, time in the daily fellowship with Himself, for Him to exercise the full influence of His presence on us, and time, day by day, in the course of our being kept waiting, for faith to prove its reality and to fill our whole being, He Himself will lead us from faith to vision; we shall see the glory of God. Let no delay shake our faith. Of faith it holds good: first the blade, then the ear, then the full corn in the ear. Each believing prayer brings a step nearer the final victory. Each believing prayer helps to ripen the fruit and bring us nearer to it; it fills up the measure of prayer and faith known to God alone; it conquers the hindrances in the unseen world; it hastens the end. Child of God, give the Father time. He is long-suffering over you. He wants the blessing to be rich, and full, and sure; give Him time, while you cry day and night. Only remember the word: "I say unto you, He will avenge them speedily."

The blessing of such persevering prayer is unspeakable. There is nothing so heart-searching as the prayer of faith. It teaches you to discover and confess, and to give up everything that hinders the coming of the blessing, everything there may be not in accordance with the Father's will. It leads to closer fellowship with Him who alone can teach us to pray, to a more entire surrender to draw nigh under no covering but that of the blood and the Spirit. It calls for a closer and more simple abiding in Christ alone. Christian, give God time. He will perfect that which concerneth you. "Long-suffering—speedily," this is God's watchword as you enter the gates of prayer: be it yours too.

Let it be thus whether you pray for yourself or for others.

All labor, bodily or mental, needs time and effort: we must give up *ourselves* to it. Nature discovers her secrets and yields her treasures only to diligent and thoughtful labor. However little we can understand it, in the spiritual husbandry it is the same: the seed we sow in the soil of heaven, the efforts we put forth, and the influence we seek to exert in the world above, need our whole being: we must *give ourselves* to prayer. But let us hold fast the great confidence that in due season we shall reap if we faint not.

And let us especially learn the lesson as we pray for the Church of Christ. She is, indeed, as the poor widow, in the absence of her Lord, apparently at the mercy of her adversary, helpless to obtain redress. Let us, when we pray for His Church or any portion of it, under the power of the world, asking Him to visit her with the mighty workings of His Spirit and to prepare her for His coming—let us pray in the assured faith: prayer does help, praying always and not fainting will bring the answer. Only give God time. And then keep crying day and night. "Hear what the unrighteous judge saith. And shall not God avenge his own elect, which cry to him day and night, and yet he is *long-suffering* over them? I say unto you, that he will avenge them speedily."

Eternity is an ever-present Now, in which the past is never past, and the future always present.

Prayer in
Harmony with God

Father, I thank thee that thou heardest me. And I knew that thou hearest me always.

JOHN 11: 41, 42.

Thou art my Son; this day have I begotten thee. Ask of me, and I shall give thee.

PSALM 2: 7, 8.

IN THE New Testament we find a distinction made between faith and knowledge. "To one is given through the Spirit the word of *wisdom;* and to another the word of *knowledge,* according to the same Spirit; to another *faith,* in the same Spirit." In a child or a simple-minded Christian there may be much faith with little knowledge. Childlike simplicity accepts the truth without difficulty, and often cares little to give itself or others any reason for its faith but this: God has said. But it is the will of God that we should love and serve Him, not only with all the heart but also with all the mind; that we should grow up into an insight into the Divine wisdom and beauty of all His ways and words and works. It is only thus that the believer will be able fully to approach and rightly to adore the glory of God's grace; and only thus that our heart can intelligently apprehend the treasures of wisdom and knowledge there are in redemption, and be prepared to enter fully into the highest note of the song that rises before the throne: "O the depth of the riches both of the wisdom and knowledge of God!"

In our prayer life this truth has its full application. While prayer and faith are so simple that the new-born convert can pray

25

with power, true Christian science finds in the doctrine of prayer some of its deepest problems. In how far is the power of prayer a reality? If it is a reality how can God grant to prayer such mighty power? How can the action of prayer be harmonized with the will and the decrees of God? How can God's sovereignty and our will, God's liberty and ours, be reconciled? These and other like questions are fit subjects for Christian meditation and inquiry. The more earnestly and reverently we approach such mysteries, the more shall we in adoring wonder fall down to praise Him who hath in prayer given such power to man.

One of the secret difficulties with regard to prayer—one which, though not expressed, does often really hinder prayer—is derived from the perfection of God, from His absolute independence of all that is outside of Himself. Is He not the Infinite Being, who owes what He is to Himself alone, who determines Himself, and whose wise and holy will has determined all that is to be? How can prayer influence Him, or He be moved by prayer to do what otherwise would not be done? Is not the promise of an answer to prayer simply a condescension to our weakness? Is what is said of the power—the much-availing power—or prayer anything more than an accommodation to our mode of thought, because the Deity never can be dependent on any action from without for its doings? And is not the blessing of prayer simply the influence it exercises upon ourselves?

In seeking an answer to such questions, we find the key in the very being of God, in the mystery of the Holy Trinity. If God was only one Person, shut up within Himself, there could be no thought of nearness to Him or influence on Him. But in God there are three Persons. In God we have Father and Son, who have in the Holy Spirit their living bond of unity and fellowship. When eternal Love begat the Son, and the Father gave the Son as the Second Person a place next Himself as His Equal and His Counsellor, a way was opened for prayer and its influence in the very inmost life of Deity itself. Just as on earth, so in heaven the whole relation between Father and Son is that of giving and taking. And if that taking is to be as voluntary and self-determined as the giving, there must be on the part of the Son an asking and receiving. In the holy fellowship of the Divine Persons, this asking of the Son was one of the great operations of the Thrice Blessed Life of God. Hence we have it in Psalm 2: "This day I have begotten thee. Ask of me, and I shall give thee." The Father gave the Son the place and the power to act on Him. The asking of the Son was no mere show or shadow, but one of those life-movements in which the love of the Father and the Son met and completed each other. The Father had determined that He should not be alone in His counsels: there was a Son on whose asking and accepting of their fulfillment should depend. And so there was in the very Being and Life of God an asking, of which prayer on earth was to be the reflection and the outflow. It was not without including this that Jesus said, "I knew that thou always hearest me." Just as the Sonship of Jesus on earth may not be separated from His Sonship in heaven, even so with His prayer on earth, it is the continuation and the counterpart of His asking in heaven. The prayer of the man Christ Jesus is the link between the eternal asking of the only begotten Son in the bosom of the Father and the prayer of men on earth. Prayer has its rise and its deepest source in the very Being of God. In the bosom of Deity nothing is ever done without prayer—the asking of the Son and the giving of the Father.*

This may help us somewhat to understand how the prayer of man, coming through the Son, can have effect on God. The decrees of God are not decisions made by Him without reference to the Son, or His petition, or the petition to be sent up through Him. By no means. The Lord Jesus is the first-begotten, the Head and Heir of all things: all things were created *through Him* and *unto Him,* and all things consist *in Him.* In the counsels of the Father, the Son, as Representative of all creation, had always a

* See this thought developed in R. Löber, *Die Lehre von Gebet.*

voice; in the decrees of the eternal purpose there was always room left for the liberty of the Son as Mediator and Intercessor, and so for the petitions of all who draw nigh to the Father in the Son.

And if the thought come that this liberty and power of the Son to act on the Father is at variance with the immutability of the Divine decrees, let us not forget that there is not with God, as there is with man, a past by which He is irrevocably bound. God does not live in time with its past and future; the distinctions of time have no reference to Him who inhabits Eternity. And Eternity is an ever-present Now, in which the past is never past, and the future always present. To meet our human weakness, Scripture must speak of past decrees, and a coming future. In reality, the immutability of God's counsel is ever still in perfect harmony with His liberty to do whatsoever He will. Not so were the prayers of the Son and His people taken up into the eternal decrees that their effect should be only an apparent one; but so that the Father-heart holds itself open and free to listen to every prayer that rises through the Son, and that God does indeed allow Himself to be decided by prayer to do what He otherwise would not have done.

This perfect harmony and union of Divine Sovereignty and human liberty is to us an unfathomable mystery, because God as *The Eternal One* transcends all our thoughts. But let it be our comfort and strength to be assured that in the eternal fellowship of the Father and the Son the power of prayer has its origin and certainty, and that through our union with the Son our prayer is taken up and can have its influence in the inner life of the Blessed Trinity. God's decrees are no iron framework against which man's liberty would vainly seek to struggle. No, God Himself is the Living Love, who in His Son as man has entered into the tenderest relation with all that is human, who through the Holy Spirit takes up all that is human into the Divine life of love, and keeps Himself free to give every human prayer its place in His government of the world.

It is in the daybreak light of such thoughts that the doctrine of the Blessed Trinity no longer is an abstract speculation, but the living manifestation of the way in which it were possible for man to be taken up into the fellowship of God, and his prayer to become a real factor in God's rule of this earth. And we can, as in the distance, catch glimpses of the light that from the eternal world shines out on words such as these: *Through him we have access by one spirit unto the Father.*

The desire for independence was the temptation in paradise, and it is the temptation in each human heart.

Like Christ: In His
Dependence on the Father

*Verily, verily, I say unto you, The Son can do nothing of himself,
but what he seeth the Father doing: for what things soever he
doeth, these the Son also doeth in like manner. For the Father
loveth the Son, and showeth him all things that himself doeth:
and greater works than these will he show him, that ye may
marvel.*

JOHN 5: 19, 20.

I know mine own, and mine own know me, even as *the Father
knoweth me, and I know the Father.*

JOHN 10: 14, 15 (R.V.)

OUR RELATION to Jesus is the exact counterpart of His to the
Father. And so the words in which He sets forth His intercourse
with the Father have their truth in us too. And as the words of
Jesus in John 5 describe the natural relation between every father
and son, whether on earth or in heaven, they are applicable not
only to the Only-begotten, but to every one who in and like Jesus
is called a son of God.

We cannot better catch the simple truth and force of the
illustration than by thinking of Jesus with His earthly father in
the carpenter's shop learning his trade. The first thing you notice
is the entire *dependence*: "The son can do nothing of himself,
but what he seeth the father doing." Then you are struck by the
implicit *obedience* that just seeks to imitate the father: "for whatsoever things the father doeth, these doeth the son in like
manner." You then notice the loving *intimacy* to which the
father admits him, keeping back none of his secrets: "for the
Father loveth the Son, and showeth him all things that himself
doeth." And in this dependent obedience on his son's part, and

31

the loving teaching on the father's part, you have the pledge of an ever-growing *advance* to greater works: step by step, the son will be led up to all that the father himself can do: "Greater works than these will he show him, that ye may marvel."

In this picture we have the reflection of the relationship between God the Father and the Son in His blessed humanity. If His human nature is to be something real and true, and if we are to understand how Christ is in very deed to be our example, we must believe fully in what our blessed Lord here reveals to us of the secrets of His inner life. The words He speaks are literal truth. His dependence on the Father for each moment of His life was absolutely and intensely real: "The Son can do nothing of himself, but what he seeth the Father doing." He counted it no humiliation to wait on His Father for His commands: He rather considered it His highest blessedness to let Himself be led and guided of the Father as a child. And, accordingly, He held Himself bound in strictest obedience to say and do only what the Father showed Him: "What things soever the Father doeth, these the Son also doeth in like manner."

The proof of this is the exceeding carefulness with which in everything He seeks to keep to Holy Scripture. In His Sufferings He will endure all in order that the Scriptures may be fulfilled. For this He remained the whole night in prayer. In such continued prayer He presents His thoughts to the Father, and waits for the answer, that He may know the Father's will. No child in his ignorance, no slave in his bondage, was ever so anxious to keep to what the father or master had said, as the Lord Jesus was to follow the teaching and guidance of His Heavenly Father. On this account the Father kept nothing hid from Him: the entire dependence and willingness always to learn were rewarded with the most perfect communication of all the Father's secrets. "For the Father loveth the Son, and showeth him all things, and will show him greater works than these, that ye may marvel." The Father had formed a glorious life plan for the Son, that in Him the Divine life might be shown forth in the conditions of human existence: this plan was shown to the Son piece by piece until at last all was gloriously accomplished.

Child of God, it is not only for the only begotten Son that a life plan has been arranged, but for each one of His children. Just in proportion as we live in more or less entire dependence on the Father will this life plan be more or less perfectly worked out in our lives. The nearer the believer comes to this entire dependence of the Son, "doing nothing but what he sees the Father do," and then to His implicit obedience, "whatsoever he doeth, doing these in like manner," so much more will the promise be fulfilled to us: "The Father showeth him all things that he himself doeth, and will show him greater works than these." Like Christ, that word calls us to a life of conformity to the Son in His blessed dependence on the Father. Each one of us is invited thus to live.

To such a life in dependence on the Father the first thing that is necessary is a firm faith that He will make known His will to us. I think this is something that keeps many back: they cannot believe that the Lord cares for them so much that He will indeed give Himself the trouble every day to teach them and to make known to them His will, just as He did to Jesus. Christian, thou art of more value to the Father than thou knowest. Thou art as much worth as the price He paid for thee, that is, the blood of His Son; He therefore attaches the highest value to the least thing that concerns thee, and will guide thee even in what is most insignificant. He longs more for close and constant intercourse with thee than thou canst conceive. He can use thee for His glory, and make something of thee, higher than thou canst understand. The Father loves His child, and shows him what He does. That He proved in Jesus, and He will prove it in us too. There must be only the surrender to expect His teaching. Through His Holy Spirit He gives this most tenderly. Without removing us from our circle, the Father can so conform us to Christ's image that we can be a blessing and joy to all. Do not let unbelief of God's compassionate love prevent us from expecting the Father's guidance in all things.

Let the unwillingness to submit yourself as little keep you back. This is the second great hindrance. The desire for independence was the temptation in paradise, and it is the temptation in each human heart. It seems hard to be nothing, to know nothing, to will nothing. And yet it is so blessed. This dependence brings us into most blessed communion with God: of us it becomes as true as of Jesus, "The Father loveth the Son, and showeth him all things whatsoever he doeth." This dependence takes from us all care and responsibility: we have only to obey orders. It gives real power and strength of will, because we know that He works in us to will and to do. It gives us the blessed assurance that our work will succeed, because we have allowed God alone to take charge of it.

My brother, if you have hitherto known but little of this life of conscious dependence and simple obedience, begin today. Let your Saviour be your example in this. It is His blessed will to live in you, and in you to be again what He was here on earth. He longs only for your acquiescence: He will work it in you. Offer yourself to the Father this day, after the example of the First-begotten, to do nothing of yourself, but only what the Father shows you. Fix your gaze on Jesus as the Example and Promise of what you shall be. Adore Him who, for your sake, humbled Himself, and showed how blessed the dependent life can be.

Blessed dependence! It is indeed the disposition which becomes us toward such a God. It gives Him the glory which belongs to Him as God. It keeps the soul in peace and rest, for it allows God to care for all. It keeps the mind quiet and prepared to receive and use the Father's teaching. And it is so gloriously rewarded in the deeper experience of holy intercourse, and the continued ever-advancing discoveries of His will and work with which the Father crowns it. Blessed dependence in which the Son lived on earth, thou art the desire of my soul!

Blessed dependence! It was because Jesus knew that He was *a Son* that He thus loved to be dependent on *the Father*. Of all the teaching in regard to the likeness to Christ this is the center and sum: I must live as a Son with my Father. If I stand clear in this relationship, *as a son realizing that the Father is everything to me,* a sonlike life, living through the Father, will be its natural and spontaneous outcome.

The love of Christ is no mere idea or sentiment; it is a real divine life power.

Like Christ:
In His Love

A new commandment I give unto you, That ye love one another; even as I have loved you, that ye also love one another.

JOHN 13: 34.

This is my commandment, that ye love one another, even as I have loved you.

JOHN 15: 12.

EVEN AS—we begin to understand somewhat of the blessedness of those little words. It is not the command of a law which only convinces of sin and impotence; it is a new command under a new covenant that is established on better promises. It is the command of Him who asks nothing that He has not provided and now offers to bestow. It is the assurance that He expects nothing from us, that He does not work in us: Even as I have loved you, and every moment am pouring out that love on you through the Holy Spirit, even so do ye love one another. The measure, the strength, and the work of your love you will find in my love to you.

Even as I have loved you: those words give us the *measure* of the love wherewith we must love each other. True love knows no measure: it gives itself entirely. It may take into consideration the time and measure of showing it; but love itself is ever whole and undivided. This is the greatest glory of Divine Love that we have, that of the Father and Son, two persons, who in love remain One Being, each losing Himself in the other. This is the glory of the love of Jesus, who is the image of God, that He loves us even as the Father loves Him. And this is the glory of

37

brotherly love, that it will know of no law other than to love even as God and Christ.

He who would be like Christ must unhesitatingly accept this as his rule of life. He knows how difficult, how impossible it often is thus to love brethren, in whom there is so much that is offensive or unamiable. Before going out to meet them in circumstances where his love may be tried, he goes in secret to the Lord, and with his eye fixed on his own sin and unworthiness asks: How much owest thou thy Lord? He goes to the cross and seeks there to fathom the love wherewith the Lord has loved him. He lets the light of the immeasurable love of Him who is in heaven, his Head and his Brother, shine in on his soul, until he learns to feel Divine Love has but one law: love seeks not its own, love gives itself wholly. And he lays himself on the altar before his Lord: even as Thou has loved me, so will I love the brethren. In virtue of my union with Jesus, and in Jesus with them, there can be no question of anything less: I love them as Christ did. Oh that Christians would close their ears to all the reasonings of their own hearts, and fix their eyes only on the law which He who loves them has promulgated in His own example; they would realize that there is nothing for them to do but this— to accept His commands and to obey them.

Our love may recognize no measure other than His, because His love is *the strength* of ours. The love of Christ is no mere idea or sentiment; it is a real divine life power. So long as the Christian does not understand this, it cannot exert its full power in him. But when his faith rises to realize that Christ's love is nothing less than the imparting of Himself and His love to the beloved, and he becomes rooted in this love as the source whence his life derives its sustenance, then he sees that his Lord simply asks that he should allow His love to flow through him. He must live in a Christ-given strength: the love of Christ constrains him, and enables him to love as He did.

From this love of Christ the Christian also learns what *the work* of his love to the brethren must be. We have already had occasion to speak of many manifestations of love: its loving service, its self-denial, its meekness. Love is the root of all these. It teaches the disciple to look on himself as really called upon to be, in his little circle, just like Jesus, the One who lives solely to love and help others. Paul prays for the Philippians: "That your love may abound more and more in knowledge and in all judgment" (Phil. 1: 9). Love does not comprehend at once what the work is that it can do. The believer who prays that his love may abound in knowledge, and really takes Christ's example as his rule of life, will be taught what a great and glorious work there is for him to do. The Church of God, and every child of God, as well as the world, have an unspeakable need of love, of the manifestation of Christ's love. The Christian who really takes the Lord's word, "Love one another, *even as* I have loved you," as a command that must be obeyed, carries about a power for blessing and life for all with whom he comes in contact. Love is the explanation of the whole wonderful life of Christ, and of the wonder of His death: Divine Love in God's children will still work its mighty wonders.

"Behold what manner of love!" "Behold how he loved!" These words are the superscription over the love of the Father and of the Son. They must yet become the keywords to the life of every Christian. They will be so where in living faith and true consecration the command of Christ to love, even as He loved, is accepted as the law of life. As early as the call of Abraham this principle was deposited as a living seed in God's kingdom, that what God is for us, we must be for others. "I will bless thee," "and thou shalt be a blessing." If "I have loved you" is the highest manifestation of what God is for us, then "Even so love ye" must be the first and highest expression of what the child of God must be. In preaching, as in the life of the Church, it must be understood: *The love which loves like Christ is the sign of true discipleship.*

Beloved Christians, Christ Jesus longs for you in order to make you, amid those who surround you, a very fountain of love.

The love of Heaven would fain take possession of you, in order that, in and through you, it may work its blessed work on earth. Yield to its rule. Offer yourself unreservedly to its indwelling. Honor it by the confident assurance that it can teach you to love as Jesus loved. As conformity to the Lord Jesus must be the chief mark of your Christian walk, so love must be the chief mark of that conformity. Be not disheartened if you do not attain it at once. Only keep fast hold of the command, "Love, even as I have loved you." It takes time to grow into it. Take time in secret to gaze on that image of love. Take time in prayer and meditation to fan the desire for it into a burning flame. Take time to survey all around you, whoever they be, and whatever may happen, with this one thought, "I must love them." Take time to become conscious of your union with your Lord, that every fear as to the possibility of thus loving may be met with the word: "Have not I commanded you: Love as I have loved"? Christian, take time in loving communion with Jesus your loving example, and you will joyfully fulfill this command, too, to love even as He did.

Nothing can atone for the loss of secret and direct intercourse with God. Even work in the service of God and of love is exhausting: we cannot bless others without power going out from us; this must be renewed from above.

Like Christ:
In His Praying

And in the morning, rising up a great while before day, he went out, and departed into a desert place, and there prayed.

MARK 1: 35.

And he saith unto them, Come ye yourselves apart into a desert place, and rest a while.

MARK 6: 31.

IN HIS LIFE of secret prayer, too, my Saviour is my example. He could not maintain the heavenly life in His soul without continually separating Himself from man, and communing with His Father. With the heavenly life in me it is not otherwise: it has the same need of entire separation from man, the need not only of single moments, but of time enough for intercourse with the Fountain of Life, the Father in Heaven.

It was at the commencement of His public ministry that the event happened which so attracted the attention of His disciples that they wrote it down. After a day full of wonders and of work at Capernaum (Mark 1: 21-32), the press in the evening became still greater. The whole town is before the door; sick are healed, and devils are cast out. It is late before they get to sleep; in the throng there is little time for quiet or for secret prayer. And, lo, as they rise early in the morning, they find Him gone. In the silence of the night He has gone out to seek a place of solitude in the wilderness; when they find Him there, He is still praying.

And why did my Saviour need these hours of prayer? Did He not know the blessedness of silently lifting up His soul to God in the midst of the most pressing business? Did not the Father dwell in Him? And did He not in the depth of His heart

43

enjoy unbroken communion with His Father? Yes, that hidden life was indeed His portion. But that life, as subject to the law of humanity, had need of continual refreshing and renewing from the fountain. It was a life of dependence; just because it was strong and true, it could not bear the loss of direct and constant intercourse with the Father, with whom and in whom it had its being and its blessedness.

What a lesson for every Christian! Much intercourse with man is dissipating, and dangerous to our spiritual life: it brings us under the influence of the visible and temporal. Nothing can atone for the loss of secret and direct intercourse with God. Even work in the service of God and of love is exhausting: we cannot bless others without power going out from us; this must be renewed from above. The law of the manna, that what is heavenly cannot remain good long on earth, but must day by day be renewed afresh from heaven, still holds good. Jesus Christ teaches it us: Every day I need time to have communion with my Father in secret. My life is like His, a life hid in heaven, in God; it needs time day by day to be fed from heaven. It is *from heaven* alone that the power to lead *a heavenly life* on earth can come.

And what may have been the prayers that occupied our Lord there so long? If I could hear Him pray, how I might learn how I, too, must pray! God be praised, of His prayers we have more than one recorded, that in them too we might learn to follow His holy example. In the high-priestly prayer (John 17) we hear Him speak, as in the deep calm of heaven, to His Father; in His Gethsemane prayer, a few hours later, we see Him call out of the depths of trouble and darkness unto God. In these two prayers we have all: the highest and the deepest that there is to be found in the communion of prayer between Father and Son.

In both these prayers we see how He addresses God. Each time it is *Father! O my Father!* In that word lies the secret of all prayer. The Lord knew that He was a Son, and that the Father loved Him: with that word He placed Himself in the full light of the Father's countenance. This was to Him the greatest need and greatest blessing of prayer, to enter into the full enjoyment of the Father's love. Let it be thus with me too. Let the principal part of my prayer be the holy silence and adoration of faith in which I wait upon God until He reveals Himself to me, and gives me, through His Spirit, the loving assurance that He looks down on me as Father, that I am well-pleasing to Him. He who in prayer has not time in quietness of soul, and in full consciousness of its meaning, to say Abba Father, has missed the best part of prayer. It is in prayer that the witness of the Spirit, that we are children of God, and that the Father draws nigh and delights in us, must be exercised and strengthened. "If our heart condemn us not, we have confidence toward God; and whatsoever we ask, we receive of him, because we obey his commandments, and do the things that are pleasing in his sight."

In both these prayers I also see what He desired: *that the Father may be glorified*. He speaks: "I have glorified thee; glorify thy Son, that thy Son *also may glorify thee*." That will assuredly have been the spirit of every prayer; the entire surrender of Himself to live only for the Father's will and glory. All that He asked had but one object, "That God might be glorified." In this, too, He is my example. I must seek to have the spirit of each prayer I offer: Father bless Thy child, and glorify Thy grace in me, only that Thy child may glorify Thee. Everything in the universe must show forth God's glory. The Christian who is inspired with this thought, and avails himself of prayer to express it, until he is thoroughly imbued with it, will have power in prayer. Even of His work in heaven our Lord says: "Whatsoever ye shall ask in my name, that will I do, *that the Father may be glorified in the Son*." O my soul, learn from thy Saviour, ere ever thou pourest out thy desires in prayer, first to yield thyself as a whole burnt-offering with the one object that God may be glorified in thee.

Then thou hast sure ground on which to pray. Thou wilt feel the strong desire, as well as the full liberty, to ask the Father that in each part of Christ's example, in each feature of Christ's image, thou mayest be made like Him, that so God may be glorified. Thou wilt understand how that only in continually renewed prayer can the soul surrender itself to wait that God may from heaven work in it what will be to His glory. Because Jesus surrendered Himself so entirely to the glory of His Father, He was worthy to be our Mediator, and could in His high-priestly prayer ask such great blessings for His people. Learn like Jesus to seek only God's glory in prayer, and thou shalt become a true intercessor, who can approach the throne of grace not only with his own needs, but also can pray for others the effectual fervent prayer of a righteous man that availeth much. The words which the Saviour put into our mouths in the Lord's Prayer: "Thy will be done," because He was made like unto His brethren in all things, He took from our lips again and made His own in Gethsemane, that from Him we might receive them back again in the power of His atonement and intercession, and so be able to pray them even as He had done. Thou, too, shalt become Christlike in that priestly intercession on which the unity and prosperity of the Church and the salvation of sinners so much depend.

And he who in every prayer makes God's glory the chief object will also, if God calls him to it, have strength for the prayer of Gethsemane. Every prayer of Christ was intercession, because He had given Himself for us; all He asked and received was in our interest; every prayer He prayed was in the spirit of self-sacrifice. Give thyself, too, wholly to God for man, and as with Jesus so with us, the entire sacrifice of ourselves to God in every prayer of daily life is the only preparation for those single hours of soul-struggle in which we may be called to some special act of the surrender of the will that costs us tears and anguish. But he who has learned the former will surely receive strength for the latter.

O my brother, if thou and I would be like Jesus we must especially contemplate Jesus praying alone in the wilderness. *There is the secret of His wonderful life.* What He did and spoke to man *was first spoken and lived through with the Father.* In communion with Him, the anointing with the Holy Spirit was each day renewed. He who would be like Him in his walk and conversation must simply begin here, that he follow Jesus into solitude. Even though it cost the sacrifice of night rest, of business, of intercourse with friends, *the time must be found to be alone with the Father.* Besides the ordinary hour of prayer, he will feel at times irresistibly drawn to enter into the holy place, and not to come thence until it has been revealed anew to him that God is his portion. In his secret chamber, with closed door, or in the solitude of the wilderness, God must be found every day, and our fellowship with Him renewed. If Christ needed it, how much more we! What it was to Him it will be for us.

What it was to Him is apparent from what is written of His baptism: "It came to pass that, Jesus also being baptized, *and praying,* the heaven was opened, and the Holy Ghost descended in a bodily shape like a dove upon him: and a voice came from heaven, which said, Thou art my beloved Son; in thee I am well pleased." Yes, this will be to us the blessing of prayer: the opened heaven, the baptism of the Spirit, the Father's voice, the blessed assurance of His love and good pleasure. *As with Jesus, so with us; from above, from above, must it all come in answer to prayer.*

Christlike praying in secret will be the secret of Christlike living in public. O let us rise and avail ourselves of our wonderful privilege—the Christlike boldness of access to the Father's presence, the Christlike liberty with God in prayer.

Be assured that when thou dost seek to use the Scriptures as Christ used them, they will do for thee what they did for Him.

Like Christ:
In His Use of Scripture

*That all things must be fulfilled, which were written in the law
of Moses, and in the prophets, and in the psalms, concerning me.*
LUKE 24: 44.

WHAT THE Lord Jesus accomplished here on earth as man He
owed greatly to His use of the Scriptures. He found in them the
way marked in which He had to walk, the food and the strength
on which He could work, the weapon by which He could overcome every enemy. The Scriptures were indeed indispensable to
Him through all His life and passion: from beginning to end
His life was the fulfillment of what had been written of Him in
the volume of the Book.

It is scarcely necessary to adduce proofs of this. In the temptation in the wilderness it was by His *"It is written"* that He conquered Satan. In His conflicts with the Pharisees He continually
appealed to the Word: *"What saith the Scripture?" "Have ye not
read?" "Is it not written?"* In His intercourse with His disciples
it was always from the Scriptures that He proved the certainty
and necessity of His sufferings and resurrection: *"How otherwise can the Scriptures be fulfilled?"* And in His intercourse
with His Father in His last sufferings it is in the words of Scripture that He pours out the complaint of being forsaken, and then
again commends His spirit into the Father's hands. All this has
a very deep meaning. He was Himself the living Word. He had
the Spirit without measure. If ever anyone, He could have done
without the written Word. And yet we see that it is everything
to Him. More than anyone else He thus shows us that *the life of
God in human flesh and the word of God in human speech* are

inseparably connected. Jesus would not have been what He was, could not have done what He did, had He not yielded Himself step by step to be led and sustained by the Word of God.

Let us try to understand what this teaches us. The Word of God is more than once called Seed; it is the seed of the Divine life. We know what seed is. It is that wonderful organism in which the life, the invisible essence of a plant or tree, is so concentrated and embodied that it can be taken away and be made available to impart the life of the tree elsewhere. This use may be twofold. As fruit we eat it, for instance, in the corn that gives us bread, and the life of the plant becomes our nourishment and our life. Or we sow it, and the life of the plant reproduces, and multiplies itself. In both aspects the Word of God is seed.

True life is found only in God. But that life cannot be imparted to us unless set before us in some shape in which we know and apprehend it. It is in the Word of God that the Invisible Divine life takes shape, and brings itself within our reach, and becomes communicable. The life, the thoughts, the sentiments, the power of God are embodied in His words. And it is only through His Word that the life of God can really enter into us. His Word is the seed of the Heavenly life.

As the bread of life we eat it, we feed on it. In eating our daily bread the body takes in the nourishment which visible nature, the sun and the earth, prepared for us in the seed corn. We assimilate it, and it becomes our very own, part of ourselves; it is our life. In feeding on the Word of God the powers of the Heavenly life enter into us, and become our very own; we assimilate them, they become a part of ourselves, the life of our life.

Or we use the seed to plant. The words of God are sown in our heart. They have a Divine power of reproduction and multiplication. The very life that is in them, the Divine thought, or disposition, or powers that each of them contains, takes roots in the believing heart and grows up; and the very thing of which the word was the expression is produced within us. The words of God are the seeds of the fulness of the Divine life.

When the Lord Jesus was made man, He became entirely dependent on the Word of God, He submitted Himself wholly to it. His mother taught it Him. The teachers of Nazareth instructed Him in it. In meditation and prayer, in the exercise of obedience and faith, He was led, during His silent years of preparation, to understand and appropriate it. The Word of the Father was to the Son the life of His soul. What He said in the wilderness was spoken from His inmost personal experience: "Man shall not live by bread alone, but by every word that proceedeth out of the mouth of God." He felt He could not live but as the Word brought Him the life of the Father. His whole life was a life of faith, a depending on the Word of the Father. The Word was to Him, not instead of the Father, but the vehicle for the living fellowship with the living God. And He had His whole mind and heart so filled with it that the Holy Spirit could at each moment find within Him, all ready for use, the right word to suggest just as he needed it.

Child of God, would you become a man of God, strong in faith, full of blessing, rich in fruit to the glory of God, be full of the Word of God, then, like Christ, make the Word your bread. Let it dwell richly in you. Have your heart full of it. Feed on it. Believe it. Obey it. It is only by believing and obeying that the Word can enter into our inward parts, into our very being. Take it day by day as the Word that proceedeth, not has proceeded, but proceedeth, is proceeding out of the mouth of God, as the Word of the living God, who in it holds living fellowship with His children, and speaks to them in living power. Take your thoughts of God's will, and God's work, and God's purpose with you, and the world, not from the Church, not from Christians around you, but from the Word taught you by the Father, and, like Christ, you will be able to fulfill all that is written in the Scripture concerning you.

In Christ's use of Scripture the most remarkable thing is this: *He found Himself there; He saw there His own image and likeness.* And He gave Himself to the fulfillment of what He found written there. It was this that encouraged Him under the bitterest sufferings, and strengthened Him for the most difficult work. Everywhere He saw traced by God's own hand the Divine waymark: *through suffering to glory.* He had but one thought: to be what the Father had said He should be, to have His life correspond exactly to the image of what He should be as He found it in the Word of God.

Disciple of Jesus, in the Scriptures *thy likeness, too, is to be found,* a picture of what the Father means thee to be. Seek to have a deep and clear impression of what the Father says in His word that thou shouldest be. If this is once fully understood, it is inconceivable what courage it will give to conquer every difficulty. To know: it is ordained of God; I have seen what has been written concerning me in God's book; I have seen the image of what I am called in God's counsel to be: this thought inspires the soul with a faith that conquers the world.

The Lord Jesus found His own image not only in the institutions, but especially in the believers of the Old Testament. Moses and Aaron, Joshua, David, and the prophets, were types. And so He is Himself again the image of believers in the New Testament. It is especially in *Him and His example* that we must find our own image in the Scriptures. "To be changed into the same image, from glory to glory, by the Spirit of the Lord," we must in the Scripture-glass gaze on that image as our own. In order to accomplish His work in us, the Spirit teaches us to take Christ as in very deed our Example, and to gaze on every feature as the promise of what we can be.

Blessed the Christian who has truly done this, who not only has found Jesus in the Scriptures, but also in His image the promise and example of what he is to become. Blessed the Christian who yields himself to be taught by the Holy Spirit not to indulge in human thoughts as to the Scriptures and what it says of believers, but in simplicity to accept what the Scriptures reveal of God's thoughts about His children.

Child of God, it was "according to the Scriptures" that Jesus

Christ lived and died; it was "according to the Scriptures" that He was raised again: all that the Scriptures said He must do or suffer He was able to accomplish because He knew and obeyed them. All that the Scriptures had promised that the Father should do for Him, the Father did. O give thyself up with an undivided heart to learn in the Scriptures what God says and seeks of thee. Let the Scriptures in which Jesus found every day the food of His life be thy daily food and meditation. Go to God's Word each day with the joyful and confident expectation that through the blessed Spirit who dwells in us the Word will indeed accomplish its Divine purpose in thee. Every word of God is full of a Divine life and power. Be assured that when thou dost seek to use the Scriptures as Christ used them, they will do for thee what they did for Him. God has marked out the plan of thy life in His Word; each day thou wilt find some portion of it there. Nothing makes a man stronger and more courageous than the assurance that he is just living out the will of God. God Himself, who had thy image portrayed in the Scriptures, will see to it that the Scriptures are fulfilled in thee, if, like His Son, thou wilt but surrender thyself to this as the highest object of thy life.

Remember that to the new heart there is a joy even sweeter than that of being forgiven, even the joy of forgiving others. The joy of being forgiven is only that of a sinner and of earth: the joy of forgiving is Christ's own joy, the joy of heaven.

Like Christ:
In Forgiving

Forbearing one another, and forgiving one another, if any man have a quarrel against any: even as *Christ forgave you,* so also do ye.

COLOSSIANS 3: 13.

IN THE LIFE of grace forgiveness is one of the first blessings we receive from God. It is also one of the most glorious. It is the transition from the old to the new life, the sign and pledge of God's love: with it we receive the right to all the spiritual gifts which are prepared for us in Christ. The redeemed saint can never forget, either here or in eternity, that he is a forgiven sinner. Nothing works more mightily to inflame his love, to awaken his joy, or to strengthen his courage, than the experience, continually renewed by the Holy Spirit as a living reality, of God's forgiving love. Every day, yes, every thought of God reminds him: I owe all to pardoning grace.

This forgiving love is one of the greatest marvels in the manifestation of the Divine nature. In it God finds His glory and blessedness. And it is in this glory and blessedness God wants His redeemed people to share, when He calls upon them, as soon and as much as they have received forgiveness, also to bestow it upon others.

Have you ever noticed how often and how expressly the Lord Jesus spoke of it? If we read thoughtfully our Lord's words in Matthew 6:12, 15; 18:21-35; Mark 11:25, we shall understand how inseparably the two are united: God's forgiveness of us and our forgiveness of others. After the Lord was ascended to grant repentance and forgiveness of sins, the Scriptures say of Him just what He had said of the Father, that we must forgive as He did. As our text expresses it, *even as Christ* has forgiven you, *so also do ye*. We must be like God, like Christ, in forgiving.

It is not difficult to find the reason for this. When forgiving love comes to us, it is not only to deliver us from punishment. No, much more; it seeks to win us for its own, to take possession of us and to dwell in us. And when thus it has come down to dwell in us it does not lose its own heavenly character and beauty: it still is forgiving love seeking to do its work, not alone toward us, but in us, and through us, leading and enabling us to forgive those who sin against us. So much so is this the case that we are told that not to forgive is a sure sign that one has himself not been forgiven. He who seeks only forgiveness from selfishness and as freedom from punishment, but has not truly accepted forgiving love to rule his heart and life, proves that God's forgiveness has never really reached him. He who, on the other hand, has really accepted forgiveness will have in the joy with which he forgives others a continual confirmation that his faith in God's forgiveness of himself is a reality. *From Christ* to receive forgiveness, and *like Christ* to bestow it on others: these two are one.

Thus the Scriptures and the Church teach: but what do the lives and experience of Christians say? Alas, how many there are who hardly know that thus it is written, or who, if they know it, think it is more than can be expected from a sinful being; or who, if they agree in general to what has been said, always find a reason, in their own particular case, why it should not be so! Others might be strengthened in evil; the offender would never forgive had the injury been done to him; there are very many eminent Christians who do not act so; such excuses are never wanting. And yet the command is so very simple, and its sanction so very solemn: "Even as Christ forgave you, so also do ye"; "If ye forgive not, neither will your Father forgive you." With such human reasoning the Word of God is made of none effect. As though it were not just through forgiving love that God seeks to conquer evil, and therefore forgives even unto seventy times seven. As though it were not plain that, not what the offender would do to me, *but what Christ has done,* must be the rule of my conduct. As though conformity to the example, not of Christ Himself, but of pious Christians, were the sign that I have truly received the forgiveness of sins.

Alas, what church or Christian circle is there in which the law of forgiving love is not grievously transgressed? How often in our Church Assemblies, in philanthropic undertakings as well as in ordinary social intercourse, and even in domestic life, proof is given that to many Christians the call to forgive, just as Christ forgave, has never yet become a ruling principle of their conduct. On account of a difference of opinion, or opposition to a course of action that appeared to us right, on the ground of a real or a fancied slight, or the report of some unkind or thoughtless word, feelings of resentment, or contempt, or estrangement, have been harbored, instead of loving, and forgiving, and forgetting like Christ. In such the thought has never yet taken possession of mind and heart, that the law of compassion and love and forgiveness, in which the relation of the head to the members is rooted, must rule the whole relation of the members to each other.

Beloved followers of Jesus, called to manifest His likeness to the world, learn that as forgiveness of your sins was one of the first things Jesus did for you, forgiveness of others is one of the first that you can do for Him. And remember that to the new heart there is a joy even sweeter than that of being forgiven, even the joy of forgiving others. The joy of being forgiven is only that of a sinner and of earth: the joy of forgiving is Christ's own joy, the joy of heaven. Oh, come and see that it is nothing less than the work that Christ Himself does, and the joy with which He Himself is satisfied, that thou art called to participate in.

It is thus that thou canst bless the world. It is as the forgiving One that Jesus conquers His enemies, and binds His friends to Himself. It is as the forgiving One that Jesus has set up His kingdom and continually extends it. It is through the same forgiving love, not only preached but *shown in the life of His disciples,* that the Church will convince the world of God's love. If the world sees men and women loving and forgiving as Jesus did, it will be compelled to confess that God is with them of a truth.

And if it still appear too hard and too high, remember that this will be only so long as we consult the natural heart. A sinful nature has no taste for this joy, and never can attain it. But in union with Christ we can do it; He who abides in Him walks even as He walked. If you have surrendered yourself to follow Christ in everything, then He will by His Holy Spirit enable you to do this too. Ere ever you come into temptation, accustom yourself to fix your gaze on Jesus, in the heavenly beauty of His forgiving love as your example: "Beholding the glory of the Lord, we are changed into the same image, from glory to glory." Every time you pray or thank God for forgiveness, make the vow that to the glory of His name you will manifest the same forgiving love to all around you. Before ever there is a question of forgiveness of others, let your heart be filled with love to Christ, love to the brethren, and love to enemies: a heart full of love finds it blessed to forgive. Let, in each little circumstance of daily life when the temptation not to forgive might arise, the opportunity be joyfully welcomed to show how truly you live in God's forgiving love, how glad you are to let its beautiful light shine through you on others, and how blessed a privilege you feel it to be thus too to bear the image of your beloved Lord.

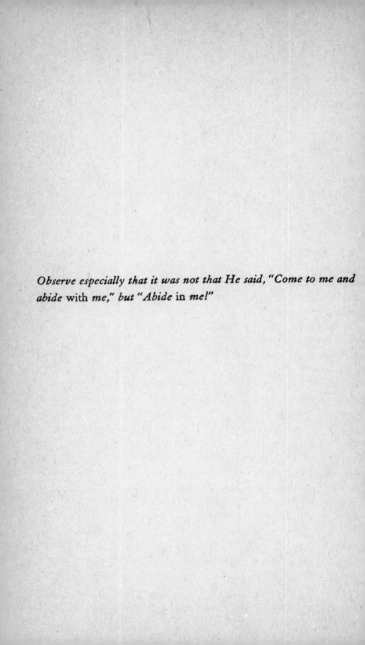

Observe especially that it was not that He said, "Come to me and abide with me," but "Abide in me!"

Abide in Christ,
All Ye Who Have Come to Him

Come unto me.
MATTHEW 11: 28.

Abide in me.
JOHN 15: 4.

IT IS to you who have heard and hearkened to the call, "*Come unto me,*" that this new invitation comes, "Abide in me." The message comes from the same loving Saviour. You doubtless have never repented having come at His call. You experienced that His word was truth; all His promises He fulfilled; He made you partakers of the blessings and the joy of His love. Was not His welcome most hearty, His pardon full and free, His love most sweet and precious? More than once, at your first coming to Him, you had reason to say, "The half was not told me."

And yet you have had to complain of disappointment: as time went on, your expectations were not realized. The blessings you once enjoyed were lost; the love and joy of your first meeting with your Saviour, instead of deepening, have become faint and feeble. And often you have wondered what the reason could be, that with such a Saviour, so mighty and so loving, your experience of salvation should not have been a fuller one.

The answer is very simple. You wandered from Him. The blessings He bestows are all connected with His, "Come to me," and are to be enjoyed only in close fellowship with Himself. You either did not fully understand, or did not rightly remember, that the call meant, "Come *to me* to stay with *me*." And yet this was in very deed His object and purpose when first He called you to

61

Himself. It was not to refresh you for a few short hours after your conversion with the joy of His love and deliverance and then to send you forth to wander in sadness and sin. He had destined you to something better than a short-lived blessedness, to be enjoyed only in times of special earnestness and prayer, and then to pass away, as you had to return to those duties in which the far greater part of life has to be spent. No, indeed; He had prepared for you an abiding dwelling with Himself, where your whole life and every moment of it might be spent, where the work of your daily life might be done, and where all the while you might be enjoying unbroken communion with Himself. It was even this He meant when to that first word, *"Come* to me," He added this, *"Abide* in me." As earnest and faithful, as loving and tender, as the compassion that breathed in that blessed *"Come"* was the grace that added this no less blessed "Abide." As mighty as the attraction with which that first word drew you were the bonds with which this second, had you but listened to it, would have kept you. And as great as were the blessings with which that coming was rewarded, so large, yea, and much greater, were the treasures to which that abiding would have given you access.

And observe especially, it was not that He said, "Come to me and abide with me," but, "Abide *in* me." The intercourse was not only to be unbroken, but most intimate and complete. He opened His arms to press you to His bosom; He opened His heart to welcome you there; He opened up all His Divine fulness of life and love, and offered to take you up into its fellowship, to make you wholly one with Himself. There was a depth of meaning you cannot yet realize in His words: "Abide *in me."*

And with no less earnestness than He had cried, "Come to me," did He plead, had you but noticed it, *"Abide in me."* By every motive that had induced you to come did He beseech you to *abide.* Was it the fear of sin and its curse that first drew you? The pardon you received on first coming could, with all the blessings flowing from it, be confirmed and fully enjoyed only in abiding in Him. Was it the longing to know and enjoy the Infinite Love that was calling you? The first coming gave but single drops to taste—'tis only the abiding that can really satisfy the thirsty soul, and give to drink of the rivers of pleasure that are at His right hand. Was it the weary longing to be made free from the bondage of sin, to become pure and holy, and so to find rest, the rest of God for the soul? This too can be realized only as you abide in Him—only abiding in Jesus gives rest in Him. Or if it was the hope of an inheritance in glory, and an everlasting home in the presence of the Infinite One: the true preparation for this, as well as its blessed foretaste in this life, are granted only to those who abide in Him. In very truth, there is nothing that moved you to come, that does not plead with thousandfold greater force: "Abide in Him." You did well to come; you do better to abide. Who would, after seeking the King's palace, be content to stand in the door when he is invited in to dwell in the King's presence and to share with Him all the glory of His royal life? Oh, let us enter in and abide, and enjoy to the full all the rich supply His wondrous love hath prepared for us!

And yet I fear that there are many who have indeed come to Jesus, and who yet have mournfully to confess that they know but little of this blessed abiding in Him. With some the reason is that they never fully understood that this was the meaning of the Saviour's call. With others, that though they heard the word, they did not know that such a life of abiding fellowship was possible, and indeed within their reach. Others will say that, though they did believe that such a life was possible, and seek after it, they have never yet succeeded in discovering the secret of its attainment. And others, again, alas, will confess that it is their own unfaithfulness that has kept them from the enjoyment of the blessing. When the Saviour would have kept them they were not found ready to stay; they were not prepared to give up everything, and always, wholly, to abide in Jesus.

To all such I come now in the name of Jesus, their Redeemer and mine, with the blessed message: "Abide in me." In His name

I invite them to come and for a season meditate with me daily on its meaning, its lessons, its claims, and its promises. I know how many, and, to the young believer, how difficult, the questions are which suggest themselves in connection with it. There is especially the question, with its various aspects, as to the possibility, in the midst of wearying work and continual distraction, of keeping up, or rather being kept in, the abiding communion. I do not undertake to remove all difficulties; this Jesus Christ Himself alone must do by His Holy Spirit. But what I would fain by the grace of God be permitted to do is, to repeat day by day the Master's blessed command, "Abide in me," until it enter the heart and find a place there, no more to be forgotten or neglected. I would fain that in the light of Holy Scripture we should meditate on its meaning, until the understanding, that gate to the heart, opens to apprehend something of what it offers and expects. So we shall discover the means of its attainment, and learn to know what keeps us from it, and what can help us to it. So we shall feel its claims, and be compelled to acknowledge that there can be no true allegiance to our King without simply and heartily accepting this one, too, of His commands. So we shall gaze on its blessedness, until desire be inflamed, and the will with all its energies be roused to claim and possess the unspeakable blessing.

Come, my brethren, and let us day by day set ourselves at His feet, and meditate on this word of His, with an eye fixed on Him alone. Let us set ourselves in quiet trust before Him, waiting to hear His holy voice—the still small voice that is mightier than the storm that rends the rocks—breathing its quickening spirit within us, as He speaks: "Abide in me." The soul that truly hears *Jesus Himself speak the word* receives with the word the power to accept and to hold the blessing He offers.

Abiding in Him is not a work that we have to do as the condition for enjoying His salvation, but a consenting to let Him do all for us, and in us, and through us.

Abide in Christ,
Trusting Him to Keep You

I follow after, if that I may apprehend that for which I also am apprehended of Christ Jesus.

PHILIPPIANS 3: 12.

MORE THAN one admits that it is a sacred duty and a blessed privilege to abide in Christ, but shrinks back continually before the question: Is a life of unbroken fellowship with the Saviour possible? Eminent Christians, to whom special opportunities of cultivating this grace have been granted, may attain to it, for the large majority of disciples, whose life, by a Divine appointment, is so fully occupied with the affairs of this life, it can scarcely be expected. The more they hear of this life, the deeper their sense of its glory and blessedness, and there is nothing they would not sacrifice to be made partakers of it. But they are too weak, too unfaithful—they never can attain to it.

Dear souls, how little they know that the abiding in Christ is just meant for the weak, and so beautifully suited to their feebleness. It is not the doing of some great thing, and does not demand that we first lead a very holy and devoted life. No, it is simply weakness entrusting itself to a Mighty One to be kept— the unfaithful one casting self on One who is altogether trustworthy and true. Abiding in Him is not a work that we have to do as the condition for enjoying His salvation, but a consenting to let Him do all for us, and in us, and through us. It is a work He does for us—the fruit and the power of His redeeming love. Our part is simply to yield, to trust, and to wait for what He has engaged to perform.

It is this quiet expectation and confidence, resting on the

67

word of Christ that *in Him* there is an abiding place prepared, which is so sadly wanting among Christians. They scarcely take the time or the trouble to realize that when He says *"Abide IN ME,"* He offers Himself, the Keeper of Israel that slumbers not nor sleeps, with all His power and love, as *the living home of the soul,* where the mighty influences of His grace will be stronger to keep than all their feebleness to lead astray. The idea they have of grace is this, that their conversion and pardon are God's work, but that now, in gratitude to God, it is their work to live as Christians and follow Jesus. There is always the thought of a work that has to be done, and even though they pray for help, still the work is theirs. They fail continually, and become hopeless; and the despondency only increases the helplessness. No, wandering one, as it was Jesus who drew thee when He spake, *"Come,"* so it is Jesus who keeps thee when He says, *"Abide."* The grace to come and the grace to abide are alike from Him alone. That word *come,* heard, meditated on, accepted, was the cord of love that drew thee nigh; that word *abide* is even so the band with which He holds thee fast and binds thee to Himself. Let the soul but take time to listen to the voice of Jesus. *"In me,"* He says, "is thy place—in my almighty arms. It is I who love thee so, who speak, *Abide in me;* surely thou canst trust me." The voice of Jesus entering and dwelling in the soul cannot but call for the response: "Yes, Saviour, *in Thee* I can, I will abide."

Abide in me: These words are no law of Moses, demanding from the sinful what they cannot perform. They are the command of love, which is ever only a promise in a different shape. Think of this until all feeling of burden and fear and despair pass away, and the first thought that comes as you hear of abiding in Jesus be one of bright and joyous hope: it is for me, I know I shall enjoy it. You are not under the law, with its inexorable *Do,* but under grace, with its blessed *Believe* what Christ will do for you. And if the question be asked, "But surely there is something for us to do?" the answer is, "Our doing and working are but the fruit of Christ's work in us." It is when the soul becomes utterly passive, looking and resting on what Christ is to do, that its energies are stirred to their highest activity, and that we work most effectually because we know that He works in us. It is as we see in that word *in me* the mighty energies of love reaching out after us to have us and to hold us, that all the strength of our will is roused to abide in Him.

This connection between Christ's work and our work is beautifully expressed in the words of Paul, "I follow after, if that *I may apprehend* that whereunto *I also am apprehended* of Christ Jesus." It was because he knew that the mighty and the faithful One had grasped him with the glorious purpose of making him one with Himself that he did his utmost to grasp the glorious prize. The faith, the experience, the full assurance, "Christ hath apprehended me," gave him the courage and the strength to press on and apprehend that whereunto he was apprehended. Each new insight of the great end for which Christ had apprehended and was holding him roused him afresh to aim at nothing less.

Paul's expression, and its application to the Christian life, can be best understood if we think of a father helping his child to mount the side of some steep precipice. The father stands above, and has taken the son by the hand to help him on. He points him to the spot on which he will help him to plant his feet as he leaps upward. The leap would be too high and dangerous for the child alone; but the father's hand is his trust, and he leaps to get hold of the point for which his father has taken hold of him. It is the father's strength that secures him and lifts him up, and so urges him to use his utmost strength.

Such is the relation between Christ and thee, O weak and trembling believer. Fix first thine eyes on the *whereunto* for which He hath apprehended thee. It is nothing less than a life of abiding, unbroken fellowship with Himself to which He is seeking to lift thee up. All that thou hast already received—pardon and peace, the Spirit and His grace—are but preliminary to this. And all that thou seest promised to thee in the future—holiness and fruitfulness and glory everlasting—are but its natural outcome. *Union with Himself,* and so with the Father, is His highest object. Fix thine eye on this, and gaze until it stand out before thee clear and unmistakable: Christ's aim is to have me abiding in Him.

And then let the second thought enter thy heart: *Unto this I am apprehended of Christ.* His almighty power hath laid hold on me, and offers now to lift me up to where He would have me. Fix thine eyes on Christ. Gaze on the love that beams in those eyes, and that asks whether thou canst not trust Him who sought and found and brought thee nigh, now to keep thee. Gaze on that arm of power, and say whether thou hast not reason to be assured that He is indeed able to keep thee abiding in Him.

And as thou thinkest of the spot whither He points—the blessed *whereunto* for which He apprehended thee—and keepest thy gaze fixed on Himself, holding thee and waiting to lift thee up, O say, couldest thou not this very day take the upward step, and rise to enter upon this blessed life of abiding in Christ? Yes, begin at once, and say, O my Jesus, if Thou biddest me, and if Thou engagest to lift and keep me there, I will venture. Trembling, but trusting, I will say: Jesus, I do abide in Thee."

My beloved fellow believer, go, and take time alone with Jesus, and say this to Him. I dare not speak to you about abiding in Him for the mere sake of calling forth a pleasing religious sentiment. God's truth must be acted on at once. O yield yourself this very day to the blessed Saviour in the surrender of the one thing He asks of you: give up yourself to abide in Him. He Himself will work it in you. You can trust Him to keep you trusting and abiding.

And if ever doubts again arise, or the bitter experience of failure tempt you to despair, just remember where Paul found His strength: "I am apprehended of Jesus Christ." In that assurance you have a fountain of strength. From that you can look up to the whereunto on which He has set His heart, and set yours there too. From that you gather confidence that the good work

He hath begun He will also perform. And in that confidence you will gather courage, day by day, afresh to say, "I follow on, that I may also apprehend that for which I am apprehended of Christ Jesus." It is because Jesus has taken hold of me, and because Jesus keeps me, that I dare to say: Saviour, I abide in Thee."

Love gives all, but asks all.

Abide in
Christ and in His Love

As the Father hath loved me so have I loved you: abide ye in my love.

JOHN 15: 9.*

Bₗₑₛₛₑ𝐃 Lₒ𝐑𝐃, enlighten our eyes to see aright the glory of this wondrous word. Open to our meditation the secret chamber of *Thy love,* that our souls may enter in, and find there their everlasting dwelling place. How else shall we know aught of a love that passeth knowledge?

Before the Saviour speaks the word that invites us to abide in His love, He first tells us what that love is. What He says of it must give force to His invitation, and make the thought of not accepting it an impossibility: *"As* the Father hath loved me, *so* have I loved you!"

"As the Father hath loved me." How shall we be able to form right conceptions of this love? Lord, teach us. God is love. Love is His very being. Love is not an attribute, but the very essence of His nature, the center around which all His glorious attributes gather. It was because He was love that He was the Father, and that there was a Son. Love needs an object to which it can give itself, in which it can lose itself, with which it can make itself one. Because God is love, there must be a Father and a Son. The love of the Father to the Son is that Divine passion with which He delights in the Son, and speaks, "My beloved Son,

* It is difficult to understand why in our English Bible one Greek word should in the first sixteen verses of John 15 have had three different translations: *abide* in verse 4, *continue* in verse 9, and *remain* in verses 11 and 16. The Revised Versions, of course, have kept the one word, *abide.* *Note:* In verse 11, the American Revised Version renders it, "May be in you."

73

in whom I am well pleased." The Divine love is as a burning fire; in all its intensity and infinity it has but one object, but one joy, and that is the only-begotten Son. When we gather together all the attributes of God—His infinity, His perfection, His immensity, His majesty, His omnipotence—and consider them but as the rays of the glory of His love, we still fail in forming any conception of what that love must be. It is a love that passeth knowledge.

And yet this love of God to His Son must serve, O my soul, as the glass in which thou art to learn how Jesus loves thee. As one of His redeemed ones, thou art His delight, and all His desire is to thee, with the longing of a love which is stronger than death, and which many waters cannot quench. His heart yearns after thee, seeking thy fellowship and thy love. Were it needed, He could die again to possess thee. As the Father loved the Son, and could not live without Him, could not be God the blessed without Him, so Jesus loves thee. His life is bound up in thine; thou art to Him inexpressibly more indispensable and precious than thou ever canst know. Thou art one with Himself. "As the Father hath loved me so have I loved you." What a love!

It is an eternal love. From before the foundation of the world —God's Word teaches us this—the purpose had been formed that Christ should be the Head of His Church, that He should have a body in which His glory could be set forth. In that eternity He loved and longed for those who had been given Him by the Father; and when He came and told His disciples that He loved them, it was, indeed, not with a love of earth and of time, but with the love of eternity. And it is with that same infinite love that His eye still rests upon each of us here seeking to abide in Him, and in each breathing of that love there is, indeed, the power of eternity. "I have loved thee with an everlasting love."

It is a perfect love. It gives all, and holds nothing back. "The Father loveth the Son, and hath given all things into His hand," and just so Jesus loves His own: all He has is theirs. When it was needed, He sacrificed His throne and crown for thee: He did not count His own life and blood too dear to give for thee. His righteousness, His Spirit, His glory, even His throne, all are thine. This love holds nothing, nothing back, but, in a manner which no human mind can fathom, makes thee one with itself. O wondrous love, to love us even as the Father loved Him, and to offer us this love as our everyday dwelling!

It is a gentle and most tender love. As we think of the love of the Father to the Son, we see in the Son everything so infinitely worthy of that love. When we think of Christ's love to us, there is nothing but sin and unworthiness to meet the eye. And the question comes, How can that love within the bosom of the Divine life and its perfections be compared to the love that rests on sinners? Can it indeed be the same love? Blessed be God, we know it is so. The nature of love is always one, however different the objects. Christ knows of no law of love but that with which His Father loved Him. Our wretchedness only serves to call out more distinctly the beauty of love, such as could not be seen even in Heaven. With the tenderest compassion He bows to our weakness, with patience inconceivable He bears with our slowness, with the gentlest loving-kindness He meets our fears and our follies. It is the love of the Father to the Son, beautified, glorified, in its condescension, in its exquisite adaptation to our needs.

And it is an unchangeable love. "Having loved his own which were in the world, he loved them to the end." "The mountains shall depart, and the hills be removed, but my kindness shall not depart from thee." The promise with which it begins its work in the soul is this: "I shall not leave thee until I have done that which I have spoken to thee of." And just as our wretchedness was what first drew it to us, so the sin, with which it is so often grieved, and which may well cause us to fear and doubt, is but a new motive for it to hold to us all the more. And why? We can give no reason but this: "As the Father hath loved me so have I loved you."

And now, does not this love suggest the *motive,* and the

measure, and the *means* of that surrender by which we yield ourselves wholly to abide in Him?

This love surely supplies a motive. Only look and see how this love stands and pleads and prays. Gaze, O gaze on the Divine form, the eternal glory, the heavenly beauty, the tenderly pleading gentleness of the crucified love, as it stretches out its pierced hands and says, "Oh, wilt thou not abide with me? Wilt thou not come and abide in me?" It points thee up to the eternity of love whence it came to seek thee. It points thee to the Cross, and all it has borne to prove the reality of its affection, and to win thee for itself. It reminds thee of all it has promised to do for thee, if thou wilt but throw thyself unreservedly into its arms. It asks thee whether, so far as thou hast come to dwell with it and taste its blessedness, it hath not done well by thee. And with a Divine authority, mingled with such an inexpressible tenderness, that one might almost think he heard the tone of reproach in it, it says, "Soul, as the Father hath loved me so have I loved you: abide in my love." Surely there can be but one answer to such pleading: Lord Jesus Christ, here I am. Henceforth, Thy love shall be the only home of my soul: in Thy love alone will I abide.

That love is not only the motive, but also the measure, of our surrender to abide in it. Love gives all, but asks all. It does so, not because it grudges us aught, but because without this it cannot get possession of us to fill us with itself. In the love of the Father and the Son it was so. In the love of Jesus to us it was so. In our entering into His love to abide there it must be so too; our surrender to it must have no measure other than its surrender to us. O that we understood how the love that calls us has infinite riches and fulness of joy for us, and that what we give up for its sake will be rewarded a hundredfold in this life! Or rather, would that we understood that it is a LOVE with a height and depth and a length and a breadth that passes knowledge! How all thought of sacrifice or surrender would pass away, and our souls be filled with wonder at the unspeakable privilege of being loved with such a love, of being allowed to come and abide in it forever!

And if doubt again suggest the question: But is it possible, can I always abide in His love? Hear how that love itself supplies the only means for abiding in Him: It is faith in that love which will enable us to abide in it. If this love be, indeed, so Divine, such an intense and burning passion, then surely I can depend on it to keep me and to hold me fast. Then surely all my unworthiness and feebleness can be no hindrance. If this love be, indeed, so Divine, with infinite power at its command, I surely have a right to trust that it is stronger than my weakness; and that with its almighty arm it will clasp me to its bosom, and suffer me to go out no more. I see how this is the one thing my God requires of me. Treating me as a reasonable being endowed with the wondrous power of willing and choosing, He cannot force all this blessedness on me, but waits till I give the willing consent of the heart. And the token of this consent He has in His great kindness ordered faith to be—that faith by which utter sinfulness casts itself into the arms of love to be saved, and utter weakness to be kept and made strong. O Infinite Love! Love with which the Father loved the Son! Love with which the Son loves us! I can trust thee, I do trust thee. O keep me abiding in Thyself.

Christ owes everything to His death and His grave.

Christ Our Life

Christ who is our life.
COLOSSIANS 3: 4.

ONE QUESTION that rises in every mind is this: "How can I live that life of perfect trust in God?" Many do not know the right answer, or the full answer. It is this: "Christ must live it in me." That is what He became man for, as a man to live a life of trust in God, and so to show to us how we ought to live. When He had done that upon earth, He went to heaven, that He might do more than show us, might give us, and live in us that life of trust. It is as we understand what the life of Christ is and how it becomes ours that we shall be prepared to desire and to ask of Him that he would live it Himself in us. When first we have seen what the life is, then we shall understand how it is that He can actually take possession, and make us like Himself. I want especially to direct attention to that first question. I wish to set before you the life of Christ as He lived it, that we may understand what it is that He has for us and that we can expect from Him. Christ Jesus lived a life upon earth that He expects us literally to imitate. We often say that we long to be like Christ. We study the traits of His character, mark His footsteps, and pray for grace to be like Him, and yet, somehow, we succeed but very little. And why? Because we are wanting to pluck the fruit while the root is absent. If we want really to understand what the imitation of Christ means, we must go to that which constituted the very root of His life before God. It was a life of absolute dependence, absolute trust, absolute surrender, and until we are one with Him in what is the principle of His life, it is in vain to seek here or there to copy the graces of that life.

79

In the Gospel story we find five great points of special importance: the birth, the life on earth, the death, the resurrection, and the ascension. In these we have what an old writer has called "the process of Jesus Christ," the process by which He became what He is today—our glorified King, and our life. In all this life process we must be made like unto Him. Look at the first. What have we to say about His birth? This: He received His life *from* God. What about His life upon earth? He lived that life in dependence *upon* God. About His death? He gave up His life *to* God. About His resurrection? He was raised from the bed *by* God. And about His ascension? He lives His life in glory *with* God.

First, He received His life from God. And why is it of consequence that we should look to that? Because Christ Jesus had in that the starting-point of His whole life. He said: "The Father sent me"; "The Father hath given the Son all things"; "The Father hath given the Son to have life in Himself." Christ received it as His own life, just as God has His life in Himself. And yet, all the time it was a life given and received. "Because the Father almighty has given this life unto me, the Son of man on earth, I can count upon God to maintain it and to carry me through all." And that is the first lesson we need. We need often to meditate on it, and to pray, and to think, and to wait before God, until our hearts open to the wonderful consciousness that the everlasting God has a divine life within us which cannot exist but through Him. I believe God has given His life; it roots in Him. I shall feel it must be maintained by Him. We often think that God has given us a life which is now our own, a spiritual life, and that we are to take charge; and then we complain that we cannot keep it right. No wonder. We must learn to live, learn to live as Jesus did. I have a God-given treasure in this earthen vessel. I have the light of the knowledge of the glory of God in the face of Christ. I have the life of God's Son within me given me by God Himself, and it can be maintained by God Himself only as I live in fellowship with Him.

What does the Apostle Paul teach us in Romans 6—there where he has just told us that we must reckon ourselves dead unto sin, and alive unto God in Christ Jesus? He goes on at once to say: "Therefore yield, present yourselves unto God, as those that are alive from the dead." How often a Christian hears solemn words about his being alive to God, and his having to reckon himself dead indeed to sin, and alive to God in Christ! He does not know what to do; he immediately casts about: "How can I keep it, this death and this life?" Listen to what Paul says. The moment that you reckon yourself dead to sin and alive to God, go with that life to God Himself, and present yourself as alive from the dead, and say to God: "Lord, Thou hast given me this life. Thou alone canst keep it. I bring it to Thee. I cannot understand all. I hardly know what I have got, but I come to God to perfect what He has begun." To live like Christ I must be conscious every moment that my life has come from God, and that He alone can maintain it.

Then, second, how did Christ live out His life during the thirty-three years in which He walked here upon earth? He lived it in dependence on God. You know how continually He says: "The Son can do nothing of himself. The words that I speak, I speak not of myself." He waited unceasingly for the teaching, and the commands, and the guidance of the Father. He prayed for power from the Father. Whatever He did, He did in the name of the Father. He, the Son of God, felt the need of much prayer, of persevering prayer, of bringing down from heaven and maintaining the life of fellowship with God in prayer. We hear a great deal about trusting God. Most blessed! And we may say: "Ah, that is what I want," and we may forget what is the very secret of all—that God, in Christ, must work all in us. I not only need God as an object of trust, but I must have Christ within as the power to trust; He must live His own life of trust in me. Look at it in that wonderful story of Paul the Apostle, the beloved servant of God. He is in danger of self-confidence, and God in heaven sends that terrible trial in Asia to bring him down, lest he trust in himself and not in the living God. God watched over his servant that he should be kept trusting. Remember that other story about the thorn in the flesh, in II Corinthians 12, and think what that means. He was in danger of exalting himself, and the blessed Master came to humble him, and to teach him: "I keep thee weak, that thou mayest learn to trust not in thyself, but in me." If we are to enter into the rest of faith, and to abide there; if we are to live the life of victory in the land of Canaan, it must begin here. We must be broken down from all self-confidence and learn like Christ to depend absolutely and unceasingly upon God. There is a greater work to be done in that than perhaps we know. We must be broken down, and the habit of our souls must be unceasingly: "I am nothing; God is all. I cannot walk before God for one hour as I should, unless God keep the life He has given me." What a blessed solution God gives, then, to all our questions and our difficulties, when He says: "My child, Christ has gone through it all for thee. Christ hath wrought out a new nature that can trust God; and Christ the Living One in heaven will live in thee, and enable thee to live that life of trust." That is why Paul said: "Such confidence have we toward God, through Christ." What does that mean? Does it mean only through Christ as the mediator, or intercessor? Verily, no. It means much more; through Christ living in and enabling us to trust God as He trusted Him.

Then comes, third, the death of Christ. What does that teach us of Christ's relation to the Father? It opens up to us one of the deepest and most solemn lessons of Christ life, one which the Church of Christ understands all too little. We know what the death of Christ means as an atonement, and we never can emphasize too much that blessed substitution and bloodshedding, by which redemption was won for us. But let us remember, that is only half the meaning of His death. The other half is this: just as much as Christ was my substitute, who died for me, just so much He is my head, in whom, and with whom, I die; and just as He lives for me, to intercede, He lives in me, to carry out and to perfect His life. And if I want to know what that life is which He will live in me, I must look at His death. By His death He proved that He possessed life only to hold it, and to spend it, for God. To the very uttermost, without the shadow of a moment's exception, He lived for God—every moment, everywhere, He held life only for His God. And so, if one wants to live a life of perfect trust, there must be the perfect surrender of his life, and his will, even unto the very death. He must be willing to go all lengths with Jesus, even to Calvary. When a boy twelve years of age Jesus said: "Wist ye not that I must be about my Father's business?" and again when He came to Jordan to be baptized: "It becometh us to fulfill all righteousness." So on through all His life, He ever said: "It is my meat and drink to do the will of my Father. I come not to do my own will, but the will of him that sent me." "Lo, I am come to do thy will, O God." And in the agony of Gethsemane, His words were: "Not my will, but thine, be done."

Someone says: "I do indeed desire to live the life of perfect trust; I desire to let Christ live it in me; I am longing to come to such an apprehension of Christ as shall give me the certainty that Christ will forever abide in me; I want to come to the full assurance that Christ, my Joshua, will keep me in the land of victory." What is needful for that? My answer is: "Take care that you do not take a false Christ, an imaginary Christ, a half Christ." And what is the full Christ? The full Christ is the man who said, "I give up everything to the death that God may be glorified. I have not a thought, I have not a wish, I would not live a moment except for the glory of God." You say at once, "What Christian can ever attain that?" Do no task that question, but ask, "Has Christ attained it and does Christ promise to live in me?" Accept Him in His fullness and leave Him to teach you how far He can bring you and what He can work in you. Make no conditions or stipulations about failure, but cast yourself upon, abandon yourself to this Christ who lived that life of utter surrender to God that He might prepare a new nature which He could impart to you and in which He might make you like Himself. Then you will be in the path by which He can lead you on to blessed experience and possession of what He can do for you. Christ Jesus came into the world with a commandment from the Father that He should lay down His life, and He lived with that one thought in His bosom His whole life long. And the one thought that ought to be in the heart of every believer is this: "I am in the death with Christ; absolutely, unchangeably given up to wait upon God, that God may work out His purpose and glory in me from moment to moment." Few attain the victory and the enjoyment and the full experience at once. But this you can do: Take the right attitude and as you look to Jesus and what He was, say: "Father, Thou hast made me a partaker of the divine nature, a partaker of Christ. It is in the life of Christ given up to Thee to the death, in His power and indwelling, in His likeness, that I desire to live out my life before Thee." Death is a solemn thing, an awful thing. In the Garden it cost Christ great agony to die that death; and no wonder it is not easy to us. But we willingly consent when we have learned the secret; in death alone the life of God will come; in death there is blessedness unspeakable. It was this that made Paul so willing to bear the sentence of death in himself; he knew the God who quickeneth the dead. The sentence of death is on everything that is of nature. But are we willing to accept it, do we cherish it? And are we not rather trying to escape the sentence or to forget it? We do not believe fully that the sentence of death is on us. Whatever is of nature must die. Ask God to make you willing to believe with your heart that to die with Christ is the only way to live in Him. You ask, "But must it, then, be dying every day?" Yes, beloved; Jesus lived every day in the prospect of the cross, and we, in the power of His victorious life, being made conformable to His death, must rejoice every day in going down with Him into death. Take an illustration. Take an oak of some hundred years' growth. How was that oak born? In a grave. The acorn was planted in the ground, a grave was made for it that the acorn might die. It died and disappeared; it cast roots downward, and it cast shoots upward, and now that tree has been standing a hundred years. Where is it standing? In its grave; all the time in the very grave where the acorn died, it has stood there stretching its roots deeper and deeper into that earth in which its grave was made, and yet, all the time, though it stood in the very grave where it had died, it has been growing higher, and stronger, and broader, and more beautiful. And all the fruit it ever bore, and all the foliage that adorned it year by year, it owed to that grave in which its roots are cast and kept. Even so, Christ owes everything to His death and His grave. And we, too, owe everything to that grave of Jesus. Oh, let us lie every day rooted in the death of Jesus. Be not afraid, but say: "To my own will I will die; to human wisdom, and human strength, and to the world I will die; for it is in the grave of my Lord that life has its beginning, and its strength and its glory."

This brings us to our next thought. First, Christ received life from the Father; second, Christ lived it in dependence on the Father; third, Christ gave it up in death to the Father; and now, fourth, Christ received it again, raised by the Father, by the power of the glory of the Father. Oh, the deep meaning of the resurrection of Christ! What did Christ do when He died? He went down into the darkness and absolute helplessness of death. He gave up a life that was without sin, a life that was God-given, a life that was beautiful and precious; and He said, "I will give it into the hands of my Father if he asks it," and He did; and He was there in the grave, waiting on God to do His will; and because He honored God to the uttermost in His helplessness, God lifted Him up to the very uttermost of glory and power. Christ lost nothing by giving up His life in death to the Father. And so, if you want the glory and the life of God to come on you, it is in the grave of utter helplessness that that life of glory will be born. Jesus was raised from the dead, and that resurrection power, by the grace of God, can and will work in us. Let no one expect to live a right life until he lives a full resurrection life in the power of Jesus. Let me state in a different way what this resurrection means.

Christ had a perfect life, given by God. The Father said: "Will you give up that life to me? Will you part with it at my command?" And Jesus parted with it, but God gave it back to Him in a second life ten thousand times more glorious than that earthly life. So God will do to every one of us who willingly consents to part with his life. Have you ever understood it? Jesus was born twice. The first time He was born in Bethlehem. That was a birth into a life of weakness. But the second time He was born from the grave; He is the "first-born from the dead." Because He gave up the life that He had by His first birth, God gave him the life of the second birth, in the glory of heaven and the throne of God. Christians, that is exactly what we need to do. A man may be an earnest Christian; a man may be a successful worker; he may be a Christian who has had a measure of growth and advance; but if he has not entered this fullness of blessing, then he needs to come to a second and deeper experience of God's saving power; he needs, just as God brought him out of Egypt, through the Red Sea, to come to a point where God brings him through Jordan into Canaan. Beloved, we have been baptized into the death of Christ. It is as we say: "I have had a very blessed life, and I have had many blessed experiences, and God has done many things for me; but I am conscious there is something wrong still; I am conscious that this life of rest and victory is not really mine." Before Christ got His life of rest and victory on the throne, He had to die and give up all. Do you it, too, and you shall share His victory and glory. It is as we follow Jesus in His death that His resurrection, power, and joy will be ours.

And then comes our last point. The fifth step in His wondrous path was: He was lifted up to be forever with the Father. Because He humbled Himself, therefore God highly exalted Him. Wherein cometh the beauty and blessedness of that exaltation of Jesus? For Himself perfect fellowship with the Father;

for others participation in the power of God's omnipotence. Yes, that was the fruit of His death. Scripture promises not only that God will, in the resurrection life, give us joy, and peace that passeth all understanding, victory over sin, and rest in God, but He will baptize us with the Holy Ghost; or, in other words, will fill us with the Holy Ghost. Jesus was lifted to the throne of heaven that He might there receive from the Father the Spirit in His new, divine manifestation, to be poured out in His fullness. And as we come to the resurrection life, the life in the faith of Him who is one with us, and sits on the throne—as we come to that, we too may be partakers of the fellowship with Christ Jesus as He ever dwells in God's presence, and the Holy Spirit will fill us, to work in us, and out of us, in a way that we have never known.

Jesus got this divine life by depending absolutely on the Father all His life long, depending on Him even down into death. Jesus got that life in the full glory of the Spirit to be poured out, by giving Himself up in obedience and surrender to God alone, and leaving God even in the grave to work out His mighty power; and that very Christ will live out His life in you and me. Oh, the mystery! Oh, the glory! and, oh, the Divine certainty. Jesus Christ means to live out that life in you and me. What think you, ought we not to humble ourselves before God? Have we been Christians so many years, and realized so little what we are? I am a vessel set apart, cleansed, emptied, consecrated; just standing, waiting every moment for God, in Christ, by the Holy Spirit, to work out in me as much of the holiness and the life of His Son as pleases Him. And until the Church of Christ comes to go down into the grave of humiliation, and confession, and shame; until the Church of Christ comes to lay itself in the very dust before God, and to wait upon God to do something new, and something wonderful, something supernatural, in lifting it up, it will remain feeble in all its efforts to overcome the world. Within the Church what lukewarmness, what worldliness, what disobedience, what sin! How can we ever fight this battle, or meet these difficulties? The answer is: Christ, the risen One, the crowned One, the almighty One, must come, and live in the individual members. But we cannot expect this except as we die with Him. I referred to the tree grown so high and beautiful, with its roots every day for a hundred years in the grave in which the acorn died. Children of God, we must go down deeper into the grave of Jesus. We must cultivate the sense of impotence, and dependence, and nothingness, until our souls walk before God every day in a deep and holy trembling. God keep us from being anything. God teach us to wait on Him, that He may work in us all He wrought in His Son, till Christ Jesus may live out His life in us! For this may God help us!

Do all God's children understand this, that holiness is just an-
other name, the true name, that God gives for happiness . . . ?

Holiness
and Happiness

The kingdom of God is joy in the Holy Ghost.

ROMANS 14: 17.

The disciples were filled with joy, and with the Holy Ghost.

ACTS 13: 52.

Then Nehemiah said, This day is holy *unto the Lord: neither be ye sorry; for the* joy *of the Lord is your strength. So the Levites stilled all the people, saying, Hold your peace; for the day is* holy; *neither be ye grieved. And all the people went their way to make great* mirth, *because they had understood the words.*

NEHEMIAH 8: 10-12.

THE DEEP significance of joy in the Christian life is hardly understood. It is too often regarded as something secondary, whereas its presence is essential as the proof that God does indeed satisfy us, and that His service is our delight. In our domestic life we do not feel satisfied if all the proprieties of deportment are observed, and each does his duty to the other; true love makes us happy in each other; as love gives out its warmth of affection, gladness is the sunshine that fills the home with its brightness. Even in suffering or poverty, the members of a loving family are a joy to each other. Without this gladness, especially, there is no true obedience on the part of the children. It is not the mere fulfillment of a command, or performance of a service, that a parent looks to; it is the willing, joyful alacrity with which it is done that makes it pleasing.

It is just so in the intercourse of God's children with their Father. Even in the effort after a life of consecration and gospel obedience, we are continually in danger of coming under the law

91

again, with its Thou shalt. The consequence always is failure. The law worketh only wrath; it gives neither life nor strength. It is only so long as we are standing in the joy of our Lord, in the joy of our deliverance from sin, in the joy of His love, and what He is for us, in the joy of His presence, that we have the power to serve and obey. It is only when made free from every master, from sin and self and the law, and only when rejoicing in this liberty, that we have the power to render service that is satisfying either to God or to ourselves. "I will see you again," Jesus said, "and your heart shall rejoice, and your joy shall no man take from you." Joy is the evidence and the condition of the abiding personal presence of Jesus.

If holiness be the beauty and the glory of the life of faith, it is manifest that here especially the element of joy may not be wanting. We have already seen how the first mention of God as the Holy One was in the song of praise on the shore of the Red Sea; how Hannah and Mary in their moments of inspiration praised God as the Holy One; how the name of the Thrice Holy in heaven comes to us in the song of the seraphs; and how before the throne both the living creatures and the conquering multitude who sing the song of the Lamb adore God as the Holy One. We are to "worship him in the beauty of holiness," "to sing praise at the remembrance of his holiness"; it is only in the spirit of worship and praise and joy that we can fully know God as holy. Much more, it is only under the inspiration of adoring love and joy that we can ourselves be made holy. It is as we cease from all fear and anxiety, from all strain and effort, and rest with singing in what Jesus is in His finished work as our sanctification, as we rest and rejoice in Him, that we shall be made partakers of His Holiness. It is the day of rest, that is, the day God has blessed, the day of blessing and gladness; and it is the day He blessed that is His holy day. Holiness and blessedness are inseparable.

But is not this at variance with the teaching of Scripture and the experience of the saints? Are not suffering and sorrow among God's chosen means of sanctification? Are not so the promises to the broken in heart, the poor in spirit, and the mourner? Are not self-denial and the forsaking of all we have, the crucifixion with Christ and the dying daily, the path to holiness? And is not all this more a matter of sorrow and pain than of joy and gladness?

The answer will be found in the right apprehension of the life of faith. Faith lifts above, and gives possession of, what is the very opposite of what we feel or experience. In the Christian life there is always a paradox; what appear irreconcilable opposites are found side by side at the same moment. Paul expresses it in the words, "As dying, and, behold, we live; as sorrowful, yet always rejoicing; as poor, yet making many rich; as having nothing, yet possessing all things." And elsewhere thus, *"When* I am weak, *then* am I strong." The apparent contradiction has its reconciliation, not only in the union of the two lives, the human and the Divine, in the person of each believer, but especially in our being, at one and the same moment, partakers of the death and the resurrection of Christ. Christ's death was one of pain and suffering, a real and terrible death, a rending asunder of the bonds that united soul and body, spirit and flesh. The power of that death works in us: we must let it work mightily if we are to live holy; for in that death He sanctified Himself, that we ourselves might be sanctified in truth. Our holiness is like His, in the death to our own will, and to all our own life. But—this we must seek to grasp—we do not approach death from the side from which Christ met it, as an enemy to be conquered, as a suffering to be borne, before the new life can be entered on. No, the believer who knows what Christ is as the Risen One, approaches death, the crucifixion of self and the flesh and the world, from the resurrection side, the place of victory, in the power of the Living Christ. When we were baptized into Christ, we were baptized into His death and resurrection as ours; and Christ Himself, the Risen Living Lord, leads us triumphantly into the experience of the power of His death. And so, to the believer who truly lives by faith, and seeks not in his own strugglings to crucify and mortify the flesh, but knows the living Lord, the deep resurrection joy never for a moment forsakes Him, but is his strength for what may appear to others to be only painful sacrifice and cross-bearing. He says with Paul, "I glory in the cross through which I have been crucified." He never, as so many do, asks Paul's question, "Who shall deliver me from the body of this death?" without sounding the joyful and trimphant answer as a present experience, "I thank God, through Jesus Christ our Lord." "Thanks be to God, which always leadeth us in triumph in Christ." It is the joy of a Present Saviour, of the experience of a perfect salvation, the joy of a resurrection life, which alone gives the power to enter deeply and fully into the death that Christ died, and yield our will and our life to be wholly sanctified to God. In the joy of that life, from which the power of the death is never absent, it is possible to say with the Apostle each moment, "As dying, and, behold, we live; as sorrowful, yet always rejoicing."

Let us seek to learn the two lessons: Holiness is essential to true happiness; happiness is essential to true holiness. If you would have joy, the fullness of joy, an abiding joy which nothing can take away, be holy as God is holy. Holiness is blessedness. Nothing can darken or interrupt our joy but sin. Whatever be our trial or temptation, the joy of Jesus of which Peter says, "in whom ye now rejoice with joy unspeakable," can more than compensate and outweigh. If we lose our joy, it must be sin. It may be an actual transgression, or an unconscious following of self or the world; it may be the stain on conscience of something doubtful, or it may be unbelief that would live by sight, and thinks more of itself and its joy than of the Lord alone: whatever it be, nothing can take away our joy but sin. If we would live lives of joy, assuring God and man and ourselves that our Lord is everything, is more than all to us, oh, let us be holy! Let us glory in Him who is our holiness: in His presence is fullness of joy. Let us live in the Kingdom which is joy in the Holy Ghost; the

Spirit of holiness is the Spirit of joy, because He is the Spirit of God. It is the saints, God's holy ones, who will shout for joy.

And happiness is essential to true holiness. If you would be a holy Christian, you must be a happy Christian. Jesus was anointed by God with "the oil of gladness," that He might give us "the oil of joy." In all our efforts after holiness the wheels will move heavily if there be not the oil of joy; this alone removes all strain and friction, and makes the onward progress easy and delightful. Study to understand the Divine worth of joy. It is the evidence of your being in the Father's presence, and dwelling in His love. It is the proof of your being consciously free from the law and the strain of the spirit of bondage. It is the token of your freedom from care and responsibility, because you are rejoicing in Christ Jesus as your Sanctification, your Keeper, and your Strength. It is the secret of spiritual health and strength, filling all your service with the childlike, happy assurance that the Father asks nothing that He does not give strength for, and that He accepts all that is done, however feebly, in this spirit. True happiness is always self-forgetful: it loses itself in the object of its joy. As the joy of the Holy Ghost fills us, and we rejoice in God the Holy One, through our Lord Jesus Christ, we lose ourselves in the adoration and worship of the Thrice Holy, we become holy. This is, even here in the wilderness, "the Highway of Holiness: the ransomed of the Lord shall come with singing; the redeemed shall walk there; everlasting joy shall be upon their heads; they shall obtain joy and gladness."

Do all God's children understand this, that holiness is just another name, the true name, that God gives for happiness; that it is, indeed, unutterable blessedness to know that God does make us holy, that our holiness is in Christ, that Christ's Holy Spirit is within us? There is nothing so attractive as joy: have believers understood that this is the joy of the Lord—to be holy? Or is not the idea of strain, and sacrifice, and sighing, of difficulty and distance so prominent, that the thought of being holy has hardly ever made the heart glad? If it has been so, let it be so no longer. "Thou shalt glory in the Holy One of Israel." Let us claim this promise. Let the believing assurance that our Loving Father, and our Beloved Lord Jesus, and the Holy Spirit, who in dovelike gentleness rests within us, have engaged to do the work and are doing it, fill us with gladness. Let us not seek our joy in what we see in ourselves of holiness: let us rejoice in the Holiness of God in Christ as ours; let us rejoice in the Holy One of Israel. So shall our joy be unspeakable and unceasing; so shall we give Him the glory.

BE YE HOLY, AS I AM HOLY

If the unity of the Spirit, the consciousness of being members one of another, be necessary in all believers, how much more must it be the mark of those who are ministers! The power of the ministry to the saints depends upon the unity of the Spirit . . .

The Ministry
of the Spirit

*Our sufficiency is of God; who also made us sufficient as ministers
of a new covenant; not of the letter, but of the spirit: for the letter killeth, but the spirit giveth life. But if the ministration of
death came with glory, how shall not rather the ministration of
the spirit be with glory?*

II CORINTHIANS 3: 5-7.

IN NONE of his Epistles does Paul expound his conception
of the Christian ministry so clearly and fully as in the second to
the Corinthians. The need of vindicating his apostleship against
detractors, the consciousness of Divine power and glory working
in him in the midst of weakness, the intense longing of his loving heart to communicate what he had to impart, stirs his soul
to its very depths, and he lays open to us the inmost secrets of the
life that makes one a true minister of Christ and His Spirit. In
our text we have the central thought: he finds his sufficiency of
strength, the inspiration and rule of all his conduct, in the fact
that he has been made a minister of the Spirit. If we take the
different passages in which mention is made of the Holy Spirit
in the first half of the Epistle,* we shall see what, in his view, the
place and work of the Holy Spirit in the ministry is, and what
the character of a ministry is under His leading and in His power.

In the Epistle, Paul will have to speak with authority. He
begins by placing himself on a level with his readers. In his first
mention of the Spirit he tells them that the Spirit that is in him
is no other than the spirit that is in them. "Now he which es-

---

* To 6: 10, where he ends the more general description of his ministry, and
returns to personal appeal.

tablisheth *us with you* in Christ, and anointed us, is God; who also sealed us, and gave us the earnest *of the Spirit* in our hearts" (1: 21, 22). The *anointing* of the believer with the Spirit, bringing him into fellowship with Christ, the anointed One, and revealing what He is to us; the *sealing,* marking him as God's own, and giving him assurance of it; the *earnest* of the Spirit, securing at once the foretaste and the fitness for the heavenly inheritance in glory: of all this he and they are together partakers. However much there was among the Corinthians that was wrong and unholy, Paul speaks to them, thinks of them, and loves them as one in Christ. "He that establisheth *us with you* in Christ, and anointed *us*"—this deep sense of unity fills his soul, comes out throughout the Epistle, and is the secret of his power. See 1: 6, 10, 2: 3: "My joy is the joy of you all"; 4: 5: "ourselves your servants"; 4: 10-12: "death worketh in us, life in you"; 4: 15: "all things are for your sakes"; 6: 11, 7: 3: "you are in our hearts to live and die with you." If the unity of the Spirit, the consciousness of being members one of another, be necessary in all believers, how much more must it be the mark of those who are ministers! The power of the ministry to the saints depends upon the unity of the Spirit; the full recognition of believers as partakers of the anointing. But to this end the minister must himself live as an anointed and sealed one, making manifest that he has the earnest of the Spirit in his heart.

The second passage is 3: 3: "Ye are an epistle of Christ ministered by us, *written with the Spirit* of the living God; not in tables of stone, but in tables that are hearts of flesh." As distinct an act of God as was the writing of the law on the tables of stone is the writing of the law of the Spirit in the new covenant, and of the name of Christ on the heart. It is a divine work, in which, as truly as God wrote of old, the Holy Spirit uses the tongue of His minister as His pen. It is this truth that needs to be restored in the ministry, not only that the Holy Spirit is needed, but that He waits to do the work, and will do it, when the right relation to Him is maintained. Paul's own experience at Corinth (Acts

18: 5-11; I Cor. 2: 3) teaches us what conscious weakness, what fear and trembling, what sense of absolute helplessness may be, or rather is, needed, if the power of God is to rest upon us. Our whole Epistle confirms this: It was as a man under sentence of death, bearing about the dying of the Lord Jesus, that the power of Christ wrought in him. The Spirit of God stands in contrast to the flesh, the world, and self, with its life and strength; it is as these are broken down, and the flesh has nothing to glory in, that the Spirit will work. Oh that every minister's tongue might be prepared for the Holy Spirit to use it as a pen wherewith He writes!

Then come the words of our text (3: 5-7) to teach us what the special characteristic is of this New Covenant ministry of the Spirit: it *"giveth life."* The antithesis, "the letter killeth," applies not only to the law of the Old Testament, but, according to the teaching of Scripture, to all knowledge which is not in the quickening power of the Spirit. We cannot insist upon it too earnestly, that, even as the law, though we know it was "spiritual," so the gospel too has its *letter*. The gospel may be preached most clearly and faithfully; it may exert a strong moral influence; and yet the faith that comes of it may stand in the wisdom of men, and not in the power of God. If there is one thing the Church needs to cry for on behalf of its ministers and students, it is that the ministry of the Spirit may be restored in its full power. Pray that God may teach them what it is personally to live in the sealing, the anointing, the earnest of the Indwelling Spirit; what it is to know that the letter killeth; what it is that the Spirit in very deed giveth life; and what, above all, the personal life is under which the ministry of the Spirit can freely work.

Paul now proceeds to contrast the two dispensations, and the different characters of those who live in them.* He points out how, as long as the mind is blinded, there is a veil on the heart which can be taken away only as we turn to the Lord. And then

---

* "Historically, I may be living in the dispensation of the Spirit, and yet practically in that of the letter."

he adds (3: 17, 18): "Now the *Lord is the Spirit;* and where *the Spirit of the Lord* is, there is liberty. But we all, with unveiled face beholding as in a mirror the glory of the Lord, are transformed into the same image, from glory to glory, even as from *the Lord the Spirit.*" It is because God "is a Spirit" that He can give the Spirit. It was when our Lord Jesus was exalted into the life of the Spirit that He became *"the Lord the Spirit,"* could give the New Testament Spirit, and in the Spirit come Himself to His people. The disciples knew Jesus long, without knowing Him as the Lord the Spirit. Paul speaks of this, too, with regard to himself (II Cor. 5: 16). There may be in the ministry much earnest gospel preaching of the Lord Jesus as the Crucified One, without the preaching of Him as the Lord the Spirit. It is only as the latter truth is apprehended, and experienced, and then preached, that the double blessing will come that Paul speaks of here: "Where the Spirit of the Lord is, is liberty." Believers will be led into the glorious liberty of the children of God (Rom. 8: 2; Gal. 5: 1, 18). "We are transformed into the same image, even as from the Lord the Spirit": then will He do the work for which He was sent—to reveal the glory of the Lord *in us;* and as we behold it, we shall be changed from glory to glory. Of the time before Pentecost it was written: "The Spirit was not yet, because Jesus was not yet glorified." But when He had been "justified in the Spirit, and received up in glory," the Spirit came forth from "the excellent glory" into our hearts, that we, with unveiled face beholding the glory of the Lord, might be changed into His likeness. What a calling! The Ministry of the Spirit to hold up the glory of the Lord to His redeemed, and to be used by His Spirit in working their transformation into His likeness, from glory to glory! "Therefore, seeing we have this ministry, we faint not." It is as the knowledge and acknowledgment of Christ as the Lord the Spirit, and of the Spirit of Christ as changing believers into His likeness, live in the Church, that the ministry among believers will be in Life and Power—in very deed a ministry of the Spirit.

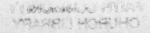

The power of the ministry on the Divine side is the Spirit; on the human, it is here, as everywhere, faith. The next mention of the Spirit is in 4: 13. *"Having the same spirit of faith."* After having, in chapter 3, set forth the glory of the Ministry of the Spirit, and, 4: 1-6, the glory of the gospel it preached, he turns to the vessels in which this treasure is. He has to vindicate his apparent weakness. But he does far more. Instead of apologizing for it, he expounds its Divine meaning and glory. He proves just how this constituted his power, because in his weakness Divine power could work. It has been so ordained "that the excellency of the power may be of God, and not of us." So his perfect fellowship with Jesus was maintained as he bore about "the putting to death of the Lord Jesus, that the life of Jesus also might be manifested in his mortal body." So there was even in his sufferings something of the vicarious element that marked his Lord's: "So then death worketh in us, but life in you." And then he adds, as the expression of the animating power that sustained him through all endurance and labor: "But having the same *Spirit of faith,"* of which we read in the Scripture, "according to that which is written, I believed, and therefore did I speak; we also believe, and therefore we also speak; knowing that he which raised up the Lord Jesus shall raise up us also with Jesus, and shall present us with you."

Faith is the evidence of things not seen. It sees the Invisible, and lives in it. Beginning with trust in Jesus, "in whom, though ye see him not, yet believing, ye rejoice," it goes on through the whole of the Christian life. Whatever is of the Spirit, is by faith. The great work of God, in opening the heart of His child to receive more of the Spirit, is to school his faith into more perfect freedom from all that is seen, and the more entire repose in God, even to the assurance that God dwelleth and worketh mightily in his weakness. For this end trials and sufferings are sent. Paul uses very remarkable language in regard to his sufferings in the first chapter (9): "We ourselves have had the sentence of death in ourselves, that we should not trust in ourselves, but in God which raiseth the dead," Even Paul was in danger of trusting in himself. Nothing is more natural; all life is confident of self, and nature is consistent with itself till it dies. For the mighty work he had to do he needed a trust in none less than the Living God, who raiseth the dead. To this God led him by giving him, in the affliction which came upon him in Asia, the sentence of death in himself. The trial of his faith was its strength. In our context he returns to this thought: the fellowship of the dying of Jesus is to him the means and the assurance of the experience of the power of Christ's life. In the spirit of this faith he speaks: "Knowing that he which raised up Jesus shall raise up us also."

It was not until Jesus had died that the Spirit of life could break forth from Him. The life of Jesus was born out of the grave: it is a life out of death. It is as we daily die, and bear about the dying of Jesus; as flesh and self are kept crucified and mortified; as we have in ourselves God's sentence of death on all that is of self and nature, that the life and the Spirit of Jesus will be manifest in us. And this is the Spirit of faith, that in the midst of weakness and apparent death it counts on God that raiseth the dead. And this is the ministry of the Spirit, when faith glories in infirmities, that the power of Christ may rest upon it. It is as our faith does not stagger at the earthiness and weakness of the vessel, as it consents that the excellency of the power shall be, not from ourselves or in anything we feel, but of God alone, that the Spirit will work in the power of the living God.

We have the same thought in the two remaining passages. In chapter 5: 5, he speaks again of *"the earnest of the Spirit"* in connection with our groaning and being burdened. And then in chapter 6: 6, the Spirit is introduced in the midst of the mention of his distresses and labors as the mark of his ministry. "In everything commending ourselves, as the ministers of God, in much patience, in afflictions, . . . *in the Holy Ghost, . . .* as dying, and yet, behold, we live; as chastened, and not killed; as sorrowful, yet always rejoicing; as poor, yet making many rich." The power of Christ in the Holy Spirit was to Paul such a living reality that the weakness of the flesh led him only the more to rejoice and to trust it. The Holy Spirit's dwelling and working in Him was consciously the secret spring and the Divine power of his ministry.

We may well ask, Does the Holy Spirit take the place in our ministry He took in Paul's? There is not a minister or member of the Church who has not a vital interest in the answer. The question is not whether the doctrine of the absolute need of the Holy Spirit's working is admitted, but whether there is given to the securing of His presence and working that proportion of the time and life, of the thought and faith of the ministry, which His place, as the Spirit of the Lord Jesus on the throne, demands. Has the Holy Spirit the place in the Church which our Lord Jesus would wish Him to have? When our hearts open to the inconceivably glorious truth that He is the Mighty Power of God, that in Him the Living Christ works through us, that He is the Presence with us of the Glorified Lord on the throne, we shall feel that the one need of the ministry and the Church is this: to wait at the footstool of the throne without ceasing for the clothing with the Power that comes from on high. The Spirit of Christ, in His love and power, in His death and life, is the Spirit of the ministry. As the ministry possesses this, it will be what the Head of the Church meant it to be, the ministry of the Spirit.

I cannot glory in a distant Jesus, from whom I am separated. When I try to do that, it is a thing of effort; I must have the help of the flesh to do it. I can truly glory only in a present Saviour whom the Holy Spirit glorifies, and reveals in His glory, within me.

The Spirit
and the Flesh

Are ye so foolish? having begun in the Spirit, *are ye now perfected in the flesh?*

GALATIANS 3: 3.

We are the circumcision, who worship by the Spirit *of God, and
glory in Christ Jesus, and have no confidence in the flesh: though
I myself might have confidence even in the flesh.*

PHILIPPIANS 3: 3, 4.

THE FLESH is the name by which Scripture designates our
fallen nature—soul and body. The soul at creation was placed
between the spiritual or Divine and the sensible or worldly, to
give to each its due, and guide them into that perfect union
which would result in man attaining his destiny, a spiritual body.
When the soul yielded to the temptation of the sensible, it broke
away from the rule of the Spirit and came under the power of
the body—it became flesh. And now the flesh is not only without
the Spirit, but even hostile to it: "the flesh lusteth against the
Spirit."

In this antagonism of the flesh to the Spirit there are two
sides. On the one hand, the flesh lusts against the Spirit in com-
mitting sin and transgressing God's law. On the other hand, its
hostility to the Spirit is no less manifested in its seeking to serve
God and do His will. In yielding to the flesh, the soul sought
itself instead of the God to whom the Spirit linked it; selfishness
prevailed over God's will; selfishness became its ruling principle.
And now, so subtle and mighty in this spirit of self, that the flesh,
not only in sinning against God, but even when the soul learns
to serve God, still asserts its power, refuses to let the Spirit alone

lead, and, in its efforts to be religious is still the great enemy that ever hinders and quenches the Spirit. It is owing to this deceitfulness of the flesh that there often takes place what Paul speaks of to the Galatians: "Having begun in the Spirit, are ye now perfected in the flesh?" Unless the surrender to the Spirit be very entire, and the holy waiting on Him be kept up in great dependence and humility, what has been begun in the Spirit very early and very speedily passes over into confidence in the flesh.

And the remarkable thing is what at first sight might appear a paradox, that just where the flesh seeks to serve God, there it becomes the strength of sin. Do we know not how the Pharisees, with their self-righteousness and carnal religion, fell into pride and selfishness, and became the servants of sin? Was it not just among the Galatians, of whom Paul asks the question about perfecting in the flesh what was begun in the Spirit, and whom he has so to warn against the righteousness of works, that the works of the flesh were so manifest, and that they were in danger of devouring one another? Satan has no more crafty device for keeping souls in bondage than inciting them to a religion in the flesh. He knows that the power of the flesh can never please God or conquer sin, and that in due time the flesh that has gained supremacy over the Spirit in the service of God will assert and maintain that same supremacy in the service of sin. It is only where the Spirit truly and unceasingly has the entire lead and rule in the life of worship that it will have the power to lead and rule in the life of practical obedience. If I am to deny self in intercourse with men, to conquer selfishness and temper and want of love, I must first learn to deny self in the intercourse with God. *There* the soul, the seat of self, must learn to bow to the Spirit, where God dwells.

The contrast between the worship in the Spirit and the trusting in the flesh is very beautifully expressed in Paul's description of the true circumcision—the circumcision of the heart—whose praise is not of men, but of God: "Who worship by the Spirit of God, and glory in Christ Jesus, and have no confidence in the flesh." Placing the glorying in Christ Jesus in the center as the very essence of the Christian faith and life, he marks, on the one hand, the great danger by which it is beset; on the other, the safeguard by which its full enjoyment is secured. Confidence in the flesh is the one thing above all others that renders the glorying in Christ Jesus of no effect; worship by the Spirit the one thing that alone can make it indeed life and truth. May the Spirit reveal to us what it is thus to glory in Christ Jesus!

That there is a glorying in Christ Jesus that is accompanied by much confidence in the flesh all history and experience teach us. Among the Galatians it was so. The teachers whom Paul opposed so earnestly were all preachers of Christ and His cross. But they preached it, not as men taught by the Spirit to know what the infinite and all-pervading influence of that cross must be, but as those who, having had the beginnings of God's Spirit, had yet allowed their own wisdom and their own thoughts to say what that cross meant, and so had reconciled it with a religion which to a very large extent was legal and carnal. And the story of the Galatian Church is repeated to this day even in the churches that are most confidently assured that they are free from the Galatian error. Just notice how often the doctrine of justification by faith is spoken of as if that were the chief teaching of the Epistle, while the doctrine of the Holy Spirit's indwelling as received by faith and our walking by the Spirit is hardly mentioned.

Christ crucified is the wisdom of God. The confidence in the flesh, in connection with the glorying in Christ, is seen in confidence in its own wisdom. Scripture is studied, and preached, and heard, and believed in, very much in the power of the natural mind, with little insistence upon the absolute need of the Spirit's personal teaching. It is seen in the absolute confidence with which men know that they have the truth, though they have it far more from human than from Divine teaching, and in the absence of that teachableness that waits for God to reveal His Truth in His own light.

Christ, through the Holy Spirit, is not only the Wisdom but the Power of God. The confidence in the flesh, along with much glorying in Christ Jesus, is to be seen and felt in so much of the work of the Christian Church in which human effort and human arrangement take a much larger place than the waiting on the Power that comes from on high. In the larger eccelsiastical organizations, in individual churches and circles, in the inner life of the heart and closet, alas how much unsuccessful effort, what oft-repeated failure, are to be traced to this one evil! There is no want of acknowledging Christ, His person and work, as our only hope, no want of giving Him the glory, and yet so much confidence in the flesh, rendering it of no effect.

Here let me ask again whether there be not many a one striving earnestly for a life in the fullness of consecration and the fullness of blessing, who will find here the secret of failure. To help such has been one of my first objects and most earnest prayers in writing this book. As in sermon or address, in book or conversation or private prayer, the fullness of Jesus was opened up to them with the possibility of a holy life in Him, the soul felt it all so beautiful and so simple that nothing could any longer keep it back. And, perhaps, as it accepted of what was seen to be so sure and so near, it entered into an enjoyment and experienced a power before unknown. But it did not last. There was a worm at its root. Vain was the search for what the cause of the discomfiture was, or the way of restoration. Frequently the only answer that could be found was that the surrender was not entire, or faith's acceptance not perfect. And yet the soul felt sure that it was ready, so far as it knew, to give up all, and it did long to let Jesus have all and to trust Him for all. It could almost become hopeless of an impossible perfection, if perfect consecration and perfect faith were to be the condition of the blessing. And the promise had been that it would all be so simple—just the life for the poor and feeble ones.

Listen, my brother, to the blessed teaching of God's word today. It was the confidence in the flesh that spoilt thy glorying in Christ Jesus. It was self doing what the Spirit alone can do; it was the soul taking the lead, in the hope that the Spirit would second its efforts, instead of trusting the Holy Spirit to lead and do all, and then waiting on Him. It was following Jesus, without the denial of self. This was the secret trouble. Come and listen to Paul as he tells of the only safeguard against this danger: "We are the circumcision, who worship by the Spirit of God, and glory in Christ Jesus, and have no confidence in the flesh." Here are the two elements of spiritual worship. The Spirit exalts Jesus, and abases the flesh. And if we would truly glory in Jesus, and have Him glorified in us, if we would know the glory of Jesus in personal and unchanging experience, free from the impotence which always marks the efforts of the flesh, we must simply learn what this worship of God by the Spirit is.

I can only repeat, once again, what it is the purpose of this whole book to set forth as God's truth from His blessed word: Glory in Christ Jesus. Glory in Him as the Glorified One who baptizeth with the Holy Spirit. In great simplicity and restfulness believe in Him as having given His own Spirit within you. Believe in that gift; believe in the Holy Spirit dwelling within you. Accept this as the secret of the life of Christ in you: the Holy Spirit is dwelling in the hidden recesses of your spirit. Meditate on it, believe Jesus and His word concerning it, until your soul bows with holy fear and awe before God under the glory of the truth: the Holy Spirit of God is, indeed, dwelling in me.

Yield yourself to His leading. We have seen that leading is not just in the mind or thoughts, but in the life and disposition. Yield yourself to God, to be guided by the Holy Spirit in all your conduct. He is promised to those who love Jesus and obey Him:

fear not to say that He knows you do love and do obey Him with your whole heart. Remember, then, what the one central object of His coming was: to restore the departed Lord Jesus to His disciples. "I will not leave you orphans," said Jesus; "I will come again to you." I cannot glory in a distant Jesus, from whom I am separated. When I try to do it, it is a thing of effort; I must have the help of the flesh to do it. I can truly glory only in a present Saviour whom the Holy Spirit glorifies, reveals in His glory, within me. As He does this, the flesh is abased, and kept in its place of crucifixion as an accursed thing: as He does it, the deeds of the flesh are made to die. And my whole religion will be: no confidence in the flesh, glorying in Christ Jesus, worship by the Spirit of God.

Beloved believers, having begun in the Spirit, continue, go on, persevere in the Spirit. Beware of, for one single moment, continuing or perfecting the work of the Spirit in the flesh. Let "no confidence in the flesh" be your battle cry; let a deep distrust of the flesh, and fear of grieving the Spirit by walking after the flesh, keep you very low and humble before God. Pray God for the spirit of revelation, that you may see how Jesus is all, and does all, and how by the Holy Spirit a Divine life indeed takes the place of your life, and Jesus is enthroned as the Keeper and Guide and Life of the soul.

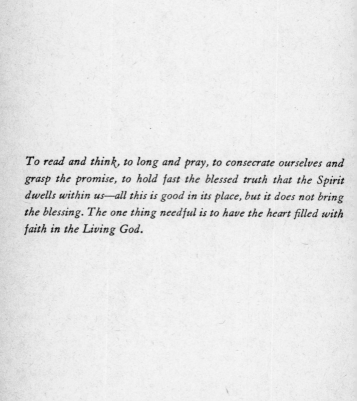

To read and think, to long and pray, to consecrate ourselves and grasp the promise, to hold fast the blessed truth that the Spirit dwells within us—all this is good in its place, but it does not bring the blessing. The one thing needful is to have the heart filled with faith in the Living God.

The Spirit through Faith

*Christ hath redeemed us from the curse, that on the Gentiles
might come* the blessing *of Abraham in Christ Jesus; that we
might receive the promise of* the Spirit through faith.
GALATIANS 3: 13, 14.

THE WORD "faith" is used the first time in Scripture in connection with Abraham. His highest praise, the secret of his
strength for obedience, and what made him so pleasing to God,
was that he believed God; and so he became the father of all
them that believe, and the great example of the blessing which
the Divine favor bestows and the path in which it comes. Just
as God proved Himself to Abraham the God who quickens the
dead, He does to us, too, in fuller measure, in giving us the Spirit
of His own Divine life to dwell in us. And just as this quickening
power came to Abraham through faith, so the blessing of Abraham, as now made manifest in Christ, even the promise of the
Spirit, is made ours by faith. All the lessons of Abraham's life
center in this: "We receive the promise of the Spirit through
faith." If we want to know what the faith is through which the
Spirit is received, how that faith comes and grows, we must study
what God has taught us of it in Abraham's story.

In Abraham's life we see what faith is: the spiritual sense by
which man recognizes and accepts the revelation of his God, a
spiritual sense called forth and awakened by that revelation. It
was because God had chosen Abraham, and determined to reveal
Himself, that Abraham became a man of faith. Each new revelation was an act of the Divine will; it is the Divine will, and the
revelation in which it carries out its purpose, that is the cause
and the life of faith. The more distinct the revelation or contact
with God, the deeper is faith stirred in the soul. Paul speaks of

115

"trust in the Living God": it is only as the Living One, in the quickening power of the Divine Life, draws nigh and touches the soul, that living faith will be called forth. Faith is not an independent act, by which in our own strength we take what God says. Nor is it an entirely passive state, in which we suffer God to do to us only what He will. But it is that receptivity of soul in which, as God comes near, and as His living Power speaks to us and touches us, we yield ourselves and accept His word and His working.

It is thus very evident that faith has two things to deal with: the Presence and the Word of the Lord. It is only the Living Presence that makes the Living Word, so that it comes not in word only but in power. It is on this account that there is so much reading and preaching of the word that bears so little fruit; so much straining and praying for faith with so little result. Men deal with the word more than with the Living God. Faith has very truly been defined as "taking God at His word." With many this has meant only, "taking the word as God's"; they did not see the force of the thought, *"Taking God* at His word." A key or a door handle has no value until I use it for the lock and the door I want to open; it is only in direct and living contact with God Himself that the word will open the heart to believe. Faith *takes God* at His word; it can do this only when and as He gives Himself. I may have in God's book all His precious promises most clear and full; I may have learned perfectly to understand how I have but to trust the promise to have it fulfilled, and yet utterly fail to find the longed-for blessing. The faith that enters on the inheritance is the attitude of soul which waits for God Himself, first, to speak His word to me, and then to do the thing He hath spoken. Faith is fellowship with God; faith is surrender to God, the impression made by His drawing nigh, the possession *He takes* of the soul by His word, holding and preparing it for His work. When once it has been awakened, it watches for every appearing of the Divine will; it listens for and accepts every indication of the Divine Presence; it looks for and expects the fulfillment of every Divine Promise.

Such was the faith through which Abraham inherited the promises. Such is the faith by which the blessing of Abraham comes upon the Gentiles in Christ Jesus, and by which we thus receive the promise of the Spirit. In all our study of the work of the Holy Spirit, and of the way in which He comes, from His first sealing us, to His full indwelling and streaming forth, let us hold fast this word: "We receive the promise of the Spirit by faith." Whether the believer be striving for the full consciousness that the Spirit dwells within, for a deeper assurance of His shedding abroad of God's love in the heart, for a larger growth of all His fruits, for the clearer experience of His guiding into all truth, or for the inducement of power to labor and to bless, let him remember that the law of faith, on which the whole economy of grace is grounded, here demands its fullest application: "According to your faith be it unto you." "We receive the promise of the Spirit by faith." Let us seek for Abraham's blessing in Abraham's faith.

In this matter let our faith begin where his began: in meeting God and waiting on God. "The Lord appeared unto Abraham. . . . And Abraham fell on his face: and God talked with him." Let us look up to our God and Father as the Living God, who is Himself, by His omnipotent quickening power, to do this wonderful thing for us: to fill us with His Holy Spirit. The blessing He has for us is the same He gave to Abraham, but larger, fuller, more wonderful. To Abraham, both when his own body was now as dead, and later on, when his son was already bound on the altar, the prey of death, He came as the Life-giving God. "He believed God, who quickeneth the dead." "He offered up Isaac, accounting God able to raise him up." To us He comes, offering to fill spirit, soul, and body with the power of a Divine life through the Holy Spirit dwelling in us. Let us be like Abraham. "Looking at the promise of God, he wavered not through unbelief, but waxed strong through faith, giving glory to God, and being fully assured that what *he* had promised, *he* was able also to perform." Let us have our souls filled with the faith of Him who has promised, our hearts fixed on Him who is able to perform: it is faith *in God* that opens the heart for God and prepares to submit to and receive His Divine working. God waits on us to fill us with His Spirit: oh, let us wait on Him. It is God who must do it all with a Divine doing, most mighty and most blessed: let us wait on Him. To read and think, to long and pray, to consecrate ourselves and grasp the promise, to hold fast the blessed truth that the Spirit dwells within us—all this is good in its place, but does not bring the blessing. The one thing needful is to have the heart filled with faith in the Living God; in that faith to abide in living contact with Him, in that faith to wait and worship before His Holy Presence. In such fellowship with God the Holy Spirit fills the heart.

When we have taken up this position, let us keep in it; we are then in the right state for the Spirit, in such measure as He already has had access to us, further revealing what God has prepared for us. As we then think of some special manifestation of the Spirit, of which the conviction of need has been wrought, or go to the promises of the word to be led into all the will of God concerning the life of the Spirit in us, we shall be kept in that humbling sense of dependence out of which childlike trust is most surely begotten. We shall be preserved from that life of strain and effort which has so often led to failure, because in the very attempt to serve God in the Spirit we were having or seeking confidence in the flesh, in something we felt, or did, or wished to do. The deep undertone of our life, in listening to the word or asking God to listen to us, in silent meditation or public worship, in work for God or daily business, will be the assurance that overtowers every other certainty: "How much more will the heavenly Father give," and will always be giving, "the Holy Spirit to them that ask him."

Such a faith will not be without its trials. Isaac, the God-given, faith-accepted life of Isaac, had to be given up to death, that it might be received back in resurrection-type, as life from the dead. The God-given experience of the Spirit's working many a time passes away, and leaves the soul apparently dull and dead. This is only until the double lesson has been fully learned; that a living faith can rejoice in a Living God, even when all feeling and experience appear to contradict the promise; and that the Divine life enters only as the life of the flesh is given to the death. The life of Christ is revealed as His death works in us, and as in weakness and nothingness we look to Him. We receive the promise of the Spirit through faith. As faith grows larger and broader, the receiving of the promised Spirit will be fuller and deeper. Each new revelation of God to Abraham made his faith stronger and his acquaintance with God more intimate. When his God drew near, he knew what to expect; he knew to trust Him even in the most unlikely appearances, as when asking the death of his son. It is the faith that waits every day on the Living God to reveal Himself, the faith that in ever-increasing tenderness of ear and readiness of service yields fully to Him and His Presence, the faith that knows that only as He wills to reveal Himself can the blessing come; but that because He always does love to reveal Himself, it will surely come—this faith that receives the promise of the Spirit.

It was in God's Presence that this faith was wakened and strengthened in Abraham and the saints of old. It was in Jesus' Presence on earth that unbelief was cast out, and that little faith became strong. It was in the Presence of the Glorified One that faith received the blessing of Pentecost. The Throne of God is now opened to us in Christ; it is become the Throne of God and the Lamb: as we tarry in humble worship, and walk in loving service before the Throne, the river of the water of life that flows from under it will flow into us, and through us, and out of us. "He that believeth, rivers of water shall flow out of him."

God is often a God that hideth Himself . . .

How It Is
to Be Found by All

*And I will sprinkle clean water upon you, and ye shall be clean:
from all your filthiness, and from all your idols, will I cleanse
you. And I will put my spirit within you, and cause you to walk
in my statutes, and ye shall keep my judgments, and do them.*
EZEKIEL 36: 25, 27.

THE FULL Pentecostal blessing is for all the children of God.
As many as are led by the Spirit of God, they are the children of
God.* God does not give a half portion to any one of His children. To every one He says: "Son, thou art ever with me, and
all that I have is thine."† Christ is not divided; he that receives
Him receives Him in all His fullness. Every Christian is destined
by God, and is actually called, to be filled with the Spirit.

I have had in view especially those who are to some extent
acquainted with these things, and have been already in search of
the truth: such as have been already led after conversion to make
a more complete renunciation of sin, and to yield themselves
wholly to the Lord. But it is quite conceivable that amongst those
who read this book there may be Christians who have heard but
little of the full Pentecostal blessing, and in whose hearts the
desire has arisen to obtain a share in it. There is, however, so
much that they do not as yet understand that they are willing
indeed to have pointed out to them, in the simplest possible
fashion, where they are to begin, and what they have to do, in
order to succeed in their desire. They are prepared to acknowledge that their life is full of sin, and that it seems to them as if

* Romans 8: 14.
† Luke 15: 31.

121

they would have to strive long and earnestly ere they can become full of the Spirit. I should like much to inspire them with fresh courage and to direct them to the God who has said: "I the Lord will hasten it in its time." * I would like to take them and guide them to the place where God will bless them, and to point to them out of His Word what the disposition and the attitude must be in which they can receive this blessing.

First of all, there must be a new discovery and confession and casting away of sin.

In the message of Ezekiel, God first promised: "I will cleanse you," then; "I will put my spirit within you." A vessel into which anything precious is to be poured must always first be cleansed. So, if the Lord is to give you a new and full blessing, a new cleansing must also take place. In your conversion, it is true, there was a confession and putting away of sin. Yet this separation was but superficial and external. The soul was still half enveloped in darkness: it thought more of its heinous sins and the punishment they might entail. After conversion it did, indeed, endeavor to overcome sin, but the effort did not succeed. It did not know in what holiness the Lord desires His people to live: it did not know how pure and holy the Lord would have it be and would make it be.

This new cleansing must come through new confession and discovery of sin. The old leaven cannot be purged away unless it be first searched for and found. Do not say that you already know sufficiently well that your Christian life is full of sin. Sit down in silent meditation and with the express purpose of seeing of what sort your life as a Christian has been. How much pride, self-seeking, worldliness, self-will, and impurity has been in it? Can such a heart receive the fullness of the Spirit? It is impossible. Look into your home life. In your intercourse with wife and children, servants and friends, do not hastiness of temper, anxiety about yourself, bitterness, idle or harsh or unbecoming

* Isaiah 9: 22.

words testify how little you have been cleansed? Look into the current life of the Church. How much religion is there that is merely intellectual, or formal, or pleasing to men, without that real humiliation of spirit, that real desire for the living God, that real love for Jesus, that real subjection to the word, which constitute worship in spirit and in truth. Look into your general course of conduct. Consider whether the people among whom you mingle can testify that they have observed, by your honorable spirit and disinterestedness and freedom from worldly-mindedness, that you are one who has been cleansed from sin by God. Contemplate all this in the light of what God expects from you and has offered to work in you, and take your place as a guilty, helpless soul that must be cleansed before God can bestow the full blessing on you.

On the back of this discovery follows the actual putting away and casting out of what is impure. This is something that you are simply bound to do. You must come with these sins, and especially with those that are most strictly your own besetting sins, and acknowledge them before God in confession, and there and then make renunciation of them. You must be brought to the conviction that your life is a guilty and shameful life. You are not at liberty to take comfort from the consideration that you are so weak, or that the majority of Christians live no higher life. It must become a matter of earnest resolve with you that your life is to undergo a complete transformation. The sins that still cleave to you are to be cast off and done away with.

Perhaps you may say in reply that you find yourself unable to do away with them or cast them off. I tell you that you are quite able to do this; and in this way: You can give these sins up to God. If there should happen to be anything in my house that I wish to have taken away, and that I myself am unable to carry, I call for men to do it for me, and I give it over into their hands, saying: "Look here: take that away"; and they do it. So I am able to say that I have put this thing out of my house. In like manner you can give up to God those sins of yours, against which you feel yourself utterly impotent. You can give them up to Him to be dealt with as He desires and He will fulfill His promise: "I will cleanse you from all your filthiness." There is nothing so needful as that there should be a very definite understanding between you and the Lord, that you on your part really confess your sin and bid it everlasting farewell and give it up, and that you wait on Him until He assures you that He has taken it, or rather has taken your heart and life, into His own hands to give you a complete victory.

In this way you come to a new discovery, and reception, and experience of what Christ is and is prepared to do for you.

If the knowledge of sin at conversion is superficial, so also is the faith in Jesus. Our faith, our reception of Jesus never goes further or deeper than our insight into sin. If since your conversion you have learned to know the inward invincible power of sin in you, you are now prepared to receive from God a discovery of the inward invincible power of the Lord Jesus in your heart, such as you have hitherto had no idea of. If you really long for a complete deliverance from sin, so as to be able to live in obedience to God, God will reveal the Lord Jesus to you as a complete Saviour. He will make you to know that, although the flesh always remains in you, with its inclination to evil, the Lord Jesus will so dwell in your heart that the power of the flesh shall be kept in subjection by Him, in order that you may no longer do the will of the flesh. Through Jesus Christ, God will cleanse you from all unrighteousness, so that day by day you may walk before God with a pure heart. What you really need is the discovery that He is prepared to work this change in you, and that you may receive it by faith, here and now.

Yes: this is what Jesus Christ desires to work in you by the Holy Spirit. He came to put away sin; not the guilt and punishment of it only, but sin itself. He has not only mastered the power and dominion of the law and its curse over you, but also has completely broken and taken away the power and dominion of sin. He has completely rescued you as a newborn soul from beneath the power of sin; and He lives in His heavenly authority and all-pervading presence in order to work out this deliverance in you. In this power He will live in you and Himself carry out His work in you. As the indwelling Christ, He is bent on maintaining and manifesting His redemption in you. The sins which you have confessed, the pride and the lovelessness, the worldly-mindedness and vanity and all uncleanness, He will by His power take out of your heart, so that, although the flesh may tempt you, the choice and the joy of your heart abide in Him and in His obedience to God's will. Yes, you may, indeed, become "more than conqueror" through Him that loved you.* As the indwelling Christ, He will overcome sin in you.

What, then, is required on our side? Only this, a thing that can be done at once, namely, that when the soul sees it to be true that Jesus will carry out this work, it shall then open the door before Him and receive Him into the heart as Lord and King. Yes, that can be done at once. A house that has remained closely shut for twenty years can be penetrated by the light in a moment if the doors and windows are thrown open. In like manner, a heart that has remained enveloped in darkness and impotence for twenty years, because it knew not that Jesus was willing to take the victory over sin into His own hands, can have its whole experience changed in a moment. When it acknowledges its sinful condition and yields itself to God, and believes that the Son of God is prepared to assume the responsibility of the inner life and its purification from sin; when it ventures to trust the Lord that He will do this work at the very moment, then it may firmly believe that it is done, and that Jesus takes all that is in me into His own hands.

This is, indeed, an act of faith that must be held fast in faith. When doors and windows are thrown open, and the light streaming in drives out the darkness, we discover at once how much dust and impurity there is in the house. But the light shines just

* Romans 8: 37.

in order that we may see how to take it away. When we receive Christ into the heart everything is not yet perfected; light and gladness are not seen and experienced at once; but by faith the soul knows that He who is faithful will keep His word and will surely do His work. The faith that has up to this moment only sought and wrestled, now rests in the Lord and His word. *It knows that what was begun by faith must be carried forward only by faith.* It says: "I abide in Jesus; I know that He abides in me and that He will manifest Himself unto me." As Jesus cleansed the lepers with a word—and it was only when they were on their way to the priest that they found out they were clean—so He cleanses us by His Word. He that firmly holds that fact in faith will see the proofs of it.

So the soul is prepared to receive the full blessing of the Spirit.

The Lord gave, first, the promise, *"I will cleanse you,"* and then the second promise, *"I will put my spirit within you."* The Holy Spirit cannot come with power or fill the heart and continue to dwell in it unless a special and complete cleansing first takes place within it. The Spirit and sin are engaged in a mortal combat. The only reason why the Spirit works so feebly in the Church is sin, which is all too little known or dreaded or cast out. Men do not believe in the power of Christ to cleanse, and therefore He cannot do His work of baptizing with the Spirit. It is from Christ that the Spirit comes, and to Christ the Spirit returns again. It is the heart that gives Christ liberty to exercise dominion in it that will inherit the full blessing. Therefore, if you have understood the lesson of this chapter, and have done what has been suggested to you; if you have believed in Jesus as the Lord who cleanses you and dwells in you to keep you clean, be assured that God will certainly fulfill His word: "I will cleanse you *and put my spirit within you.*" Cleave to Jesus, who cleanses you: let Him be all within you; God will see to it that you are filled with the Spirit.

Only keep in view these two truths:

First, that the gift and the blessing and the fullness of the Spirit do not always come, as on the day of Pentecost, with external observation. God is often a God that hideth Himself: do not be surprised, therefore, if your heart does not at once feel as you would like it to feel immediately after your act of surrender or appropriation. Rest assured that, if you fully trust Christ to do everything for you, He there and then begins to do it in secret by His Spirit. Count upon it that, if you present yourself to God as a pure vessel, cleansed by Christ, to be filled with the Spirit, God will take you at your word and say unto you: "Receive ye the Holy Spirit; be it unto you according to your faith." * At that moment bow down before Him, more and more silently, more and more deeply, in holy adoration and expectation, in the blessed assurance that the unseen God has now begun to carry on His work more mightily in you, and that He will also manifest it to you more gloriously than ever before.

The other thing you must keep in view is the purpose for which the Spirit is given. "I will put my spirit within you, and *cause you to walk in my statutes, and ye shall keep my judgments, and do them.*" The fullness of the Spirit must be sought and received and kept with the direct aim that you shall now simply and wholly live to do God's will and work upon the earth —yes, only to be able to live like the Lord Jesus, and to say with Him: "Lo, I come to do thy will." † If you cherish this disposition, the fullness of the Spirit may be positively expected. Be full of courage and yield yourself to walk in God's statutes and to keep His judgments and do them, and you may trust God to keep His word that *He will cause you* to keep and do them. He, the living God, will work in you. Even before you are aware how the Spirit is in you, He will enable you to experience the full blessing.

Have you never yet known the fullness of the Spirit, or have you perhaps been really seeking it for a long while without find-

* John 20: 22.
† Psalm 40: 7, 8; Hebrews 10: 7.

ing it? Here you have at last the sure method of winning it. Acknowledge the sinfulness of your condition as a Christian and make renunciation of it, once and for all, by yielding it up to God. Acknowledge that the Lord Jesus is ready and able to cleanse your heart from its sin, to conquer these sins by His entrance into it, and to set you free; and that His purpose is to do this at once. Take Him now as your Lord, at once and forever. Then you may be assured that God will put His Spirit within you in a way and a measure and a power of which you have hitherto had no idea. Be assured that He will do it. O permit Him to begin; let Him do it in you now.

Just as there is but one God, who is a Spirit, who hears prayer, there is but one spirit of acceptable prayer.

In the Name of Christ

Whatsoever ye shall ask in my name, *that will I do. If ye shall
ask anything in my name, I will do it. I have appointed you, that
whatsoever ye shall ask of the Father in my name, He may give
it you.*

JOHN 14: 13, 14.

*Verily, verily I say unto you, whatsoever ye shall ask the Father
in my name, he will give it you. Hitherto have ye asked nothing
in my name; ask, and ye shall receive, that your joy may be full.
At that day ye shall ask in my name.*

JOHN 16: 23, 24, 26.

IN MY NAME—repeated six times. Our Lord knew how slow
our hearts would be to take it in, and He so longed that we
should really believe that His Name is the power to which every
knee should bow, and in which every prayer could be heard,
that He did not weary of saying it over and over: *In my name!*
Between the wonderful *whatsoever ye shall ask,* and the Divine
I will do it, the Father will give it, this one word is the simple
link: *In my name.* Our asking and the Father's giving are to be
equally in the Name of Christ. Everything in prayer depends
upon our apprehending this—*In my name.*

We know what a name is: a word by which we call up to our
mind the whole being and nature of an object. When I speak of
a lamb or a lion, the name at once suggests the different nature
peculiar to each. The Name of God is meant to express His
whole Divine nature and glory. And so the Name of Christ
means His whole nature, His person and work, His disposition
and Spirit. To ask in the Name of Christ is to pray in union with
Him. When first a sinner believes in Christ, he knows and thinks
only of His merit and intercession. And to the very end that

131

is the one foundation of our confidence. And yet, as the believer grows in grace and enters more deeply and truly into union with Christ, that is, as he abides in Christ, he learns that to pray in the Name of Christ also means in His Spirit, and in the possession of His nature, as the Holy Spirit imparts it to us. As we grasp the meaning of the words, *"At that day* ye shall ask in my name"—the day when in the Holy Spirit Christ came to live in His disciples—we shall no longer be staggered at the greatness of the promise: *"Whatsoever* ye shall ask in my name, I will do it." We shall get some insight into the unchangeable necessity and certainty of the law: what is asked in the Name of Christ, in union with Him, out of His nature and Spirit, must be given. As Christ's prayer-nature lives in us, His prayer-power becomes ours too. Not that the measure of our attainment or experience is the ground of our confidence, but the honesty and whole-heartedness of our surrender to all that we see that Christ seeks to be in us will be the measure of our spiritual fitness and power to pray in His Name. "If ye abide in me," He says, "ye shall ask what ye will." As we live in Him, we get the spiritual power to avail ourselves of His Name. As the branch wholly given up to the life and service of the vine can count upon all its sap and strength for its fruit, so the believer, who in faith has accepted the fullness of the Spirit to possess his whole life, can, indeed, avail himself of all the power of Christ's Name.

Here on earth Christ as man came to reveal what prayer is. To pray in the Name of Christ we must pray as He prayed on earth; as He taught us to pray; in union with Him, as He now prays in heaven. We must in love study, and in faith accept, Him as our Example, our Teacher, our Intercessor.

Prayer in Christ on earth and in us cannot be two different things. Just as there is but one God, who is a Spirit, who hears prayer, there is but one spirit of acceptable prayer. When we realize what time Christ spent in prayer, and how the great events of His life were all connected with special prayer, we learn the necessity of absolute dependence on and unceasing direct communication with the heavenly world, if we are to live a heavenly life, or to exercise heavenly power around us. We see how foolish and fruitless the attempt must be to do work for God and heaven, without, in the first place, in prayer getting the life and the power of heaven to possess us. Unless this truth lives in us, we cannot avail ourselves aright of the mighty power of the Name of Christ. His example must teach us the meaning of His Name.

Of His baptism we read, "Jesus having been baptized, *and praying,* the heaven was opened." It was in prayer heaven was opened to Him, that heaven came down to Him with the Spirit and the voice of the Father. In the power of these He was led into the wilderness, in fasting and prayer to have them tested and fully appropriated. Early in His ministry Mark records (1: 35), "And in the morning, a great while before day, he rose and departed into a desert place, *and there prayed."* And somewhat later Luke tells (5: 15, 16), "Multitudes came together to hear and to be healed. *But he withdrew himself into the deserts, and prayed."* He knew how the holiest service, preaching and healing, can exhaust the spirit; how too much intercourse with men could cloud the fellowship with God; how time, time, full time, is needed if the spirit is to rest and root in Him; how no pressure of duty among men can free from the absolute need of much prayer. If anyone could have been satisfied with always living and working in the spirit of prayer, it would have been our Master. But He could not; He needed to have His supplies replenished by continual and long-continued seasons of prayer. To use Christ's Name in prayer surely includes this, to follow His example and to pray as He did.

Of the night before choosing His apostles we read (Luke 6: 12), "He went out into the mountain *to pray, and continued all night in prayer to God."* The first step toward the constitution of the Church, and the separation of men to be His witnesses and successors, called Him to special long-continued prayer. All had to be done according to the pattern on the mount. "The Son can do nothing of himself: the Father showeth him all things that himself doeth." It was in the night of prayer it was shown Him.

In the night between the feeding of the five thousand, when Jesus knew that they wanted to take Him by force and make Him king, and the walking on the sea, "he withdrew again into the mountain, himself alone, *to pray*" (Matt. 14: 23; Mark 6: 46; John 6: 15). It was God's will He was to come to do, and God's power He was to show forth. He had it not as a possession of His own; it had to be prayed for and received from above. The first announcement of His approaching death, after He had elicited from Peter the confession that He was the Christ, is introduced by the words (Luke 9: 15), "And it came to pass that *he was praying alone.*" The introduction to the story of the Transfiguration is (Luke 9: 28), "He went up into the mountain *to pray.*" The request of the disciples, "Lord, teach us to pray" (Luke 11: 1), follows on, "It came to pass *as he was praying* in a certain place." In His own personal life, in His intercourse with the Father, in all He is and does for men, the Christ whose name we are to use, is a man of prayer. It is prayer that gives Him His power of blessing, and transfigures His very body with the glory of heaven. It is His own prayer-life that makes Him the teacher of others how to pray. How much more must it be prayer, prayer alone, much prayer, that can fit us to share His glory of a transfigured life, or make us the channel of heavenly blessing and teaching to others. To pray in the Name of Christ is to pray as He prays.

As the end approaches, it is still more prayer. When the Greeks asked to see Him, and He spoke of His approaching death, He prayed. At Lazarus' grave He prayed. In the last night He prayed His prayer as our High Priest, that we might know what His sacrifice would win, and what His everlasting intercession on the throne would be. In Gethsemane He prayed His prayer as Victim, the Lamb giving itself to the slaughter. On the Cross it is still all prayer—the prayer of compassion for His murderers; the prayer of atoning suffering in the thick darkness; the prayer in death of confiding resignation of His spirit to the Father.

Christ's life and work, His suffering and death—it was all prayer, all dependence on God, trust in God, receiving from God, surrender to God. Thy redemption, O believer, is a redemption wrought out by prayer and intercession: thy Christ is a praying Christ: the life He lived for thee, the life He lives in thee, is a praying life that delights to wait on God and receive all from Him. To pray in His Name is to pray as He prayed. Christ is our only example because He is our Head, our Saviour, and our Life. In virtue of His Deity and of His Spirit He can live in us: we can pray in His Name, because we abide in Him and He in us.

Christ was what He taught. All His teaching was just the revelation of how He lived, and—praise God—of the life He was to live in us. His teaching of the disciples was first to awaken desire, and so prepare them for what He would by the Holy Spirit be and work in them. Let us believe very confidently: all He was in prayer, and all He taught, He Himself will give. He came to fulfill the law; much more will He fulfill the gospel in all He taught us, as to what to pray and how.

What to pray. It has sometimes been said that direct petitions, as compared with the exercise of fellowship with God, are but a subordinate part of prayer, and that "in the prayer of those who pray best and most, they occupy but an inconsiderable place." If we carefully study all that our Lord spoke of prayer, we shall see that this is not His teaching: in the Lord's Prayer, in the parables on prayer, in the illustration of a child asking bread, of our seeking and knocking, in the central thought of the prayer of faith. "Whatsoever ye pray, believe that ye have received"—in the oft-repeated *"whatsoever"* of the last evening—everywhere our Lord urges and encourages us to offer definite petitions, and to expect definite answers. It is only because we have confined prayer too much to our own needs that it has been thought needful to free it from the appearance of selfishness by giving the petitions a subordinate place. If once, believers were to awake to the glory of the work of intercession, and to see that in it, and in the definite pleading for definite gifts on definite spheres and persons, lie our highest fellowship with our glorified Lord, and our only real power to bless men, it would be seen that there can be no truer fellowship with God than these definite petitions and their answers, by which we become the channel of His grace and life to men. Then our fellowship with the Father is even such as the Son has in His intercession.

How to pray. Our Lord taught us to pray in secret, in simplicity, with the eye on God alone; in humility, in the spirit of forgiving love. But the chief truth He reiterated was ever this: to pray in faith. And he defined that faith not only as a trust in God's goodness or power, but as the definite assurance that we have received the very thing we ask. And then, in view of the delay in the answer, He insisted on perseverance and urgency. We must be followers of those "who through faith and patience inherit the promises"—the faith that accepts the promise, and knows it has what it has asked—the patience that obtains the promise and inherits the blessing. We shall then learn to understand why God, who promises to avenge His elect speedily, bears with them in seeming delay. It is that their faith may be purified from all that is of the flesh, and tested and strengthened to become that spiritual power that can do all things—can even cast mountains into the heart of the sea.

We have gazed on Christ in His prayers; we have listened to His teaching as to how we must pray; to know fully what it is to pray in His Name, we must know Him too in His heavenly intercession.

Just think what it means: that all His saving work wrought from heaven is still carried on, just as on earth, in unceasing communication with, and direct intercession with the Father, who worketh all in all, who is All in All. Every act of grace in Christ has been preceded by, and owes its power to, intercession. God has been honored and acknowledged as its Author. On the throne of God Christ's highest fellowship with the Father, and His partnership in His rule of the world, is in intercession. Every blessing that comes down to us from above bears upon it the stamp from God: through Christ's intercession. His intercession is nothing but the fruit and the glory of His atonement. When He gave Himself a sacrifice to God for men He proved that His whole heart had the one object: the glory of God in the salvation of men. In His intercession this great purpose is realized: He glorifies the Father by asking and receiving all of Him; He saves men by bestowing what He has obtained from the Father. Christ's intercession is the Father's glory, His own glory, our glory.

And now, this Christ, the Intercessor, is our life; He is our Head, and we are His body; His Spirit and life breathe in us. As in heaven so on earth, intercession is God's chosen, God's only channel of blessing. Let us learn from Christ what glory there is in it, what the way to exercise this wondrous power, what the part it is to take in work for God.

The glory of it. By it, beyond anything, we glorify God. By it we glorify Christ. By it we bring blessing to the Church and the world. By it we obtain our highest nobility—the God-like power of saving men.

The way to it. Paul writes, "Walk in love, even as Christ loved us, and gave himself a sacrifice to God for us." If we live as Christ lived, we will, as He did, give ourselves, for our whole life, to God, to be used by Him for men. When once we have done this, given ourselves, no more to seek anything for ourselves, but for men, and that to God, for Him to use us, and to impart to us what we can bestow on others, intercession will become to us, as it is in Christ in heaven, the great work of our life. And if ever the thought comes that the call is too high, or the work too great, the faith in Christ, the Interceding Christ, who lives in us, will give us the victory. We will listen to Him who said, "The works that I do, shall ye do; and greater works shall ye do." We shall remember that we are not under the law, with its impotence, but under grace with its omnipotence, working all in us. We shall believe again in Him who said to us, Rise and walk, and gave us —and we received it—His life as our strength. We shall claim afresh the fullness of God's Spirit as His sufficient provision for our need, and count Him to be in us the Spirit of Intercession, who makes us one with Christ in His. Oh, let us only keep our place—giving up ourselves, like Him, in Him, to God for men.

Then shall we understand the part intercession is to take in God's work through us. We shall no longer try to work for God, and ask Him to follow it with His blessing. We shall do what the friend at midnight did, what Christ did on earth, and ever does in heaven—we shall first get from God, and then turn to men to give what He gave us.

Servants of Christ, children of God, be of good courage! Let no fear of feebleness or poverty make you afraid—ask in the Name of Christ. His Name is Himself, in all His perfection and power. He is the living Christ, and will Himself make His Name a power in you. Fear not to plead the Name; His promise is a threefold cord that cannot be broken. *Whatsoever ye ask—in my Name*—IT SHALL BE DONE UNTO YOU.

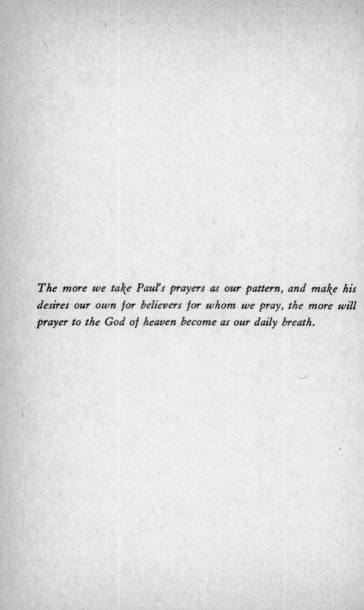

The more we take Paul's prayers as our pattern, and make his desires our own for believers for whom we pray, the more will prayer to the God of heaven become as our daily breath.

Paul,
a Pattern of Prayer

*Go and inquire for one called Saul, of Tarsus: for, behold, he
prayeth.*

ACTS 9: 11.

*For this cause I obtained mercy, that in me first Jesus Christ
might show forth all long-suffering, for a pattern to them which
should hereafter believe on him to life everlasting.*

TIMOTHY 1: 16.

GOD TOOK His own Son, and made Him our example and our
pattern. Sometimes it is as if the power of Christ's example is lost
in the thought that He, in whom is no sin, is not man as we are.
Our Lord took Paul, a man of like passions with ourselves, and
made him a pattern of what He could do for one who was the
chief of sinners. And Paul, the man who, more than any other,
has set his mark on the Church, has ever been appealed to as a
pattern man. In his mastery of Divine truth, and his teaching of
it; in his devotion to his Lord and his self-consuming zeal in his
Lord's service; in his deep experience of the power of the indwelling Christ and the fellowship of His cross; in the sincerity
of his humility and the simplicity and boldness of his faith; in his
missionary enthusiasm and endurance—in all this, and so much
more, "the grace of our Lord Jesus was exceeding abundant in
him." Christ gave him, and the Church has accepted him, as a
pattern of what Christ would have, of what Christ would work.
Seven times Paul speaks of believers following him: (I Cor. 4:
16) "Wherefore I beseech you, be ye followers of me"; (11: 1)

"Be ye followers of me, even as I am of Christ"; (Phil. 3: 17, 4: 9; I Thess. 1: 6; II Thess. 3: 7, 9).

If Paul, as a pattern of prayer, is not as much studied or appealed to as he is in other respects, it is not because he is not in this too as remarkable a proof of what grace can do, or because we do not, in this respect, as much stand in need of the help of his example. A study of Paul as a pattern of prayer will bring a rich reward of instruction and encouragement. The words our Lord used of him at his conversion, "Behold he prayeth," may be taken as the keynote of his life. The heavenly vision which brought him to his knees ever after ruled his life. Christ at the right hand of God, in whom we are blessed with all spiritual blessings, was everything to him; to pray and expect the heavenly power in his work and on his work, from heaven direct by prayer was the simple outcome of his faith in the Glorified One. In this, too, Christ meant him to be a pattern, that we might learn that, just in the measure in which the heavenliness of Christ and His gifts, the unworldliness of the powers that work for salvation, are known and believed, will prayer become the spontaneous rising of the heart to the only source of its life. Let us see what we know of Paul.

These are revealed almost unconsciously. He writes (Rom. 1: 9, 11), "God is my witness, that without ceasing I make mention of you *always in my prayers.* For I long to see you, that I may impart unto you some spiritual gift, to the end ye may be established"; (Rom. 10: 1, 9: 2, 3) "My *heart's desire and prayer to God* for Israel is, that they may be saved"; "I have great heaviness and *continual sorrow of heart;* for I could wish that myself were accursed from Christ for my brethren"; (I Cor. 1: 4) "I thank my God always on your behalf, for the grace of God which is given you by Jesus Christ"; (II Cor. 6: 4, 6) "Approving ourselves as the ministers of Christ, *in watchings, in fastings";* (Gal. 4: 19) "My little children, of whom *I travail in birth again* till Christ be formed in you"; (Eph. 1: 16) *"I cease not* to give thanks for you, making mention of you *in my prayers";* (Eph. 3:

14, 16) *"I bow my knees* to the Father, that he would grant you to be strengthened with might by his Spirit in the inner man"; (Phil. 1: 3, 4, 8, 9) "I thank my God *upon every remembrance of you, always in every prayer of mine* making request for you all with joy. For God is my record, how greatly I long after you all in the bowels of Jesus Christ. And this *I pray . . .*"; (Col. 1: 3, 9) "We give thanks to God, *praying always for you.* For this cause also, since the day we heard it, *we do not cease to pray for you,* and to desire . . ."; (Col. 2: 1) "I would that ye knew what *great conflict* I have for you, and for as many as have not seen my face in the flesh"; (I Thess. 1: 2) "We give thanks to God *always* for you all, making mention of you *in our prayers";* (3: 9, 10) "We joy for your sakes before God; *night and day praying exceedingly* that we might perfect that which is lacking in your faith"; (II Thess. 1: 3, 11) "We are bound to thank God *always* for you. Wherefore also *we always pray* for you"; (II Tim. 1: 3) "I thank God, that *without ceasing* I have remembrance of thee night and day"; (Philem. 1: 4) "I thank my God, making mention of thee *always in my prayers."*

These passages taken together give us the picture of a man whose words, "Pray without ceasing," were simply the expression of his daily life. He had such a sense of the insufficiency of simple conversion; of the need of the grace and the power of heaven being brought down for the young converts in prayer; of the need of much and unceasing prayer, day and night, to bring it down; of the certainty that prayer would bring it down, that his life was continual and most definite prayer. He had such a sense that everything must come from above, and such a faith that it would come in answer to prayer, that prayer was neither a duty nor a burden, but the natural turning of the heart to the only place whence it could possibly obtain what it sought for others.

It is of as much importance to know *what* Paul prayed as how frequently and earnestly he did so. Intercession is a spiritual work. Our confidence in it will depend much on our knowing that we ask according to the will of God. The more distinctly we ask heavenly things, which we feel at once God alone can bestow, which we are sure He will bestow, the more direct and urgent will our appeal be to God alone. The more impossible the things are that we seek, the more we will turn from all human work to prayer and to God alone.

In the Epistles, in addition to expressions in which he speaks of his praying, we have a number of distinct prayers in which Paul gives utterance to his heart's desire for those to whom he writes. In these we see that his first desire was always that they might be "established" in the Christian life. Much as he praised God when he heard of conversion, he knew how feeble the young converts were, and how for their establishing nothing would avail without the grace of the Spirit prayed down. If we notice some of his principal prayers we shall see what he asked and obtained.

Take the two prayers in Ephesians—the one for light, the other for strength. In the former (1: 15-19), he prays for the Spirit of wisdom to enlighten them to know what their calling was, what their inheritance, what the mighty power of God working in them. Spiritual enlightenment and knowledge was their great need, to be obtained for them by prayer. In the latter (3: 15, 19) he asks that the power they had been led to see in Christ, might work in them, and they be strengthened with Divine might, so as to have the indwelling Christ, and the love that passeth knowledge, and the fullness of God actually come on them. These were things that could only come direct from heaven; these were things he asked and expected. If we want to learn Paul's art of intercession, we must ask nothing less for believers in our days.

Look at the prayer in Philippians (1: 9-11). There, too, it is first for spiritual knowledge; then comes a blameless life, and then a fruitful life to the glory of God. So also in the beautiful prayer in Colossians (1: 9-11). First, spiritual knowledge and understanding of God's will, then the strengthening with all might to all patience and joy.

Or take the two prayers in I Thessalonians (3: 12, 13, and 5: 23). The one: "God so increase your love to one another, that he may stablish your *hearts unblamable in holiness.*" The other: "God *sanctify you wholly,* and preserve you blameless." The very words are so high that we hardly understand, still less believe, still less experience what they mean. Paul so lived in the heavenly world, he was so at home in the holiness and omnipotence of God and His love, that such prayers were the natural expression of what he knew God could and would do. "God stablish your hearts unblamable in holiness," "God sanctify you wholly"—the man who believes in these things and desires them, will pray for them for others. The prayers are all a proof that he seeks for them the very life of heaven on earth. No wonder that he is not tempted to trust in any human means, but looks for it from heaven alone. Again I say, the more we take Paul's prayers as our pattern, and make his desires our own for believers for whom we pray, the more will prayer to the God of heaven become as our daily breath.

These are no less instructive than his own prayers for the saints. They prove that he does not count prayer any special prerogative of an apostle; he calls the humblest and simplest believer to claim his right. They prove that he does not think that only the new converts or feeble Christians need prayer; he himself is, as a member of the body, dependent upon his brethren and their prayers. After he had preached the gospel for twenty years, he still asks for prayer that he may speak as he ought to speak. Not once for all, not for a time, but day by day, and that without ceasing, must grace be sought and brought down from heaven for his work. United, continued waiting on God is to Paul the only hope of the Church. With the Holy Spirit, a heavenly life, the life of the Lord in heaven, entered the world; nothing but unbroken communication with heaven can keep it up.

Hear how he asks for prayer, and with what earnestness (Rom. 15: 30, 31): "*I beseech you,* brethren, for the Lord Jesus Christ's sake, and for the love of the Spirit, that ye *strive to-*

gether with me in your prayers to God for me; that I may be delivered from them which do not believe in Judea; and may come unto you with joy by the will of God." How remarkably both prayers (Rom. 15: 5, 6, 13) were answered. The remarkable fact that the Roman world power, which in Pilate with Christ, in Herod with Peter, at Philippi, had proved its antagonism to God's kingdom, all at once becomes Paul's protector, and secures him a safe convoy to Rome, can be accounted for only by these prayers.

II Corinthians 1: 10, 11: "In whom we trust that he will yet deliver us; *ye also helping together by prayer* for us." Ephesians 6: 18-20: "Praying always with all prayer and supplication in the Spirit for all saints, *and for me* that I may open my mouth boldly, that therein I may speak boldly as I ought to speak." Philippians 1: 19: "I know that this [trouble] shall turn to my salvation *through your prayer,* and the supply of the Spirit of Jesus Christ." Colossians 4:2-4: "Continue in prayer, withal also *praying for us,* that God would open unto us a door of utterance, to speak the mystery of Christ, that I may make it manifest as I ought to speak." I Thessalonians 5: 25: "Brethren, pray for us." Philemon 22: "I trust that through your prayers I shall be given to you."

We saw how Christ prayed, and taught His disciples to pray. We see how Paul prayed, and taught the churches to pray. As the Master, so the servant calls us to believe and to prove that prayer is the power alike of the ministry and the Church. Of his faith we have a summary in these remarkable words concerning something that caused him grief: "This shall turn to my salvation through your prayer, and the supply of the Spirit of Jesus Christ." As much as he looked to his Lord in heaven did he look to his brethren on earth to secure the supply of that Spirit for him. The Spirit from heaven and prayer on earth were to him, as to the twelve after Pentecost, inseparably linked. We speak often of apostolic zeal and devotion and power—may God give us a revival of apostolic prayer.

In all His instructions, our Lord Jesus spoke much oftener to His disciples about their praying than their preaching. In the farewell discourse He said little about preaching, but much about the Holy Spirit, and their asking whatsoever they would in His Name. If we are to return to this life of the first apostles and of Paul, and really accept the truth every day—my first work, my only strength, is intercession, to secure the power of God on the souls entrusted to me—we must have the courage to confess past sin, and to believe that there is deliverance. To break through old habits, to resist the clamor of pressing duties that have always had their way, to make every other call subordinate to this one, whether others approve or not, will not be easy at first. But the men or women who are faithful will not only have a reward themselves, but become benefactors to their brethren. "Thou shalt be called the repairer of the breach, the restorer of paths to dwell in."

But is it really possible? Can it indeed be that those who have never been able to face, much less to overcome, the difficulty, can yet become mighty in prayer? Tell me, was it really possible for Jacob to become Israel—a prince who prevailed with God? It was. The things that are impossible with men are possible with God. Have you not in very deed received from the Father, as the great fruit of Christ's redemption, the spirit of supplication, the spirit of intercession? Just pause and think what that means. And will you still doubt whether God is able to make you "strivers with God," princes who prevail with Him? Oh, let us banish all fear, and in faith claim the grace for which we have the Holy Spirit dwelling in us, the grace of supplication, the grace of intercession. Let us quietly, perseveringly believe that He lives in us, and will enable us to do our work. Let us in faith not fear to accept and yield to the great truth that intercession, as it is the great work of the King on the throne, *is the great work of His servants on earth*. We have the Holy Spirit, who brings the Christ-life into our hearts, to fit us for this work. Let us at once begin and stir up the gift within us. As we set aside each day our time for intercession, and count upon the Spirit's enabling power, the confidence will grow that we can, in our measure, follow Paul even as he followed Christ.

Obedience to God's will shows itself in tender regard for the voice of conscience. This holds good with regard to eating and drinking, sleeping and resting, spending money and seeking pleasure . . .

On Learning Obedience

If ye love me, keep my commandments.
JOHN 14: 15.

FIRST, let me warn against a misunderstanding of the expression—"learning obedience."

We are apt to think that absolute obedience as a principle—obedience unto death—is a thing that can be learned only gradually in Christ's school. This is a great and most hurtful mistake. What we have to learn, and do learn gradually, is the practice of obedience to new and more difficult commands. But as to the principle, Christ wants us from the very entrance into His school to make the vow of entire obedience.

A little child of five can be as implicitly obedient as a youth of eighteen. The difference between the two lies, not in the principle, but in the nature of the work demanded.

Though externally Christ's obedience unto death came at the end of His life, the spirit of His obedience was the same from the beginning. Wholehearted obedience is not the end, but the beginning of our school life. The end is fitness for God's service, when obedience has placed us fully at God's disposal. A heart yielded to God in unreserved obedience is the one condition of progress in Christ's school, and of growth in the spiritual knowledge of God's will.

Young Christian, do get this matter settled at once. Remember God's rule: all for all. Give Him all: He will give you all. Consecration avails nothing unless it means presenting yourself as a living sacrifice to do nothing but the will of God. The vow of entire obedience is the entrance fee for him who would be en-

151

rolled by no assistant teacher, but by Christ Himself, in the school of obedience.

This unreserved surrender to obey, as it is the first condition of entering Christ's school, is the only fitness for receiving instruction as to the will of God for us.

There is a general will of God for all His children, which we can, in some measure, learn out of the Bible. But there is a special individual application of these commands—God's will concerning each of us personally, which only the Holy Spirit can teach. And He will not teach it except to those who have taken the vow of obedience.

This is the reason why there are so many unanswered prayers for God to make known His will. Jesus said, "If any man *wills* to do his will, he shall know of the teaching, whether it be of God." If a man's will is really set on doing God's will, that is, if his heart is given up to do, and he as a consequence does it so far as he knows it, he shall know what God has further to teach him.

It is simply what is true of every scholar with the art he studies, of every apprentice with his trade, of every man in business—doing is the one condition of truly knowing. And so obedience, the doing of God's will so far as we know, and the will and the vow to do it all as He reveals it, is the spiritual organ, the capacity for receiving the true knowledge of what is God's will for each of us.

In connection with this let me press upon you three things:

1. *Seek to have a deep sense of your very great ignorance of God's will, and of your impotence by any effort to know it aright.*

The consciousness of ignorance lies at the root of true teachableness. "The meek will he guide in the way"—those who humbly confess their need of teaching. Head-knowledge gives only human thoughts without power. God by His Spirit gives a living knowledge that enters the love of the heart, and works effectually.

2. *Cultivate a strong faith that God will make you know wisdom in the hidden part, in the heart.*

You may have known so little of this in your Christian life hitherto that the thought appears strange. Learn that God's working, the place where He gives His life and light, is in the heart, deeper than all our thoughts. Any uncertainty about God's will makes a joyful obedience impossible. Believe most confidently that the Father is willing to make known what He wants you to do. Count upon Him for this. Expect it certainly.

3. In view of the darkness and deceitfulness of the flesh and fleshly mind, *ask God very earnestly for the searching and convincing light of the Holy Spirit.*

There may be many things which you have been accustomed to think lawful or allowable, which your Father wants different. To consider it settled that they are the will of God because others and you think so may effectually shut you out from knowing God's will in other things. Bring everything, without reserve, to the judgment of the Word, explained and applied by the Holy Spirit. Wait on God to lead you to know that everything you are and do is pleasing in His sight.

There is one of the deeper and more spiritual aspects of this truth to which I have not alluded. It is something that as a rule does not come up in the early stages of the Christian life, and yet it is needful that every believer know what the privileges are that await him. There is an experience into which wholehearted obedience will bring the believer, in which he will know that, as surely as with his Lord, obedience leads to death.

Let us see what this means. During our Lord's life His resistance to sin and the world was perfect and complete. And yet His final deliverance from their temptations and His victory over their power, His obedience, was not complete until He had died to the earthly life and to sin. In that death He gave up His life in perfect helplessness into the Father's hands, waiting for Him to raise Him up. It was through death that He received the fullness of His new life and glory. Through death alone, the giving up of the life He had, could obedience lead Him into the glory of God.

The believer shares with Christ in this death to sin. In regeneration he is baptized by the Holy Spirit into it. Because of ignorance and unbelief, he may know little experimentally of this entire death to sin. When the Holy Spirit reveals to him what he possesses in Christ, and he appropriates it in faith, the Spirit works in him the very same disposition which animated Christ in His death. With Christ it was an entire ceasing from His own life, a helpless committal of His spirit into the Father's hands. This was the complete fulfillment of the Father's command: Lay down Thy life in my hands. Out of the perfect self-oblivion of the grave He entered the glory of the Father.

It is into the fellowship of this a believer is brought. He finds that in the most unreserved obedience for which God's Spirit fits him there is still a secret element of self and self-will. He longs to be delivered from it. He is taught in God's Word that this can be only by death. The Spirit helps him to claim more fully that he is, indeed, dead to sin in Christ, and that the power of that death can work mightily in him. He is made willing to be obedient unto death, this entire death to self, which makes him truly nothing. In this he finds a full entrance into the life of Christ.

To see the need of this entire death to self, to be made willing for it, to be led into the entire self-emptying and humility of our Lord Jesus—this is the highest lesson that our obedience has to learn, this is, indeed, the Christlike obedience unto death.

There is no room here to enlarge on this. I thought it well to say this much on a lesson which God Himself will, in due time, teach those who are entirely faithful.

In regard to the knowledge of God's will, we must see and give conscience its place and submit to its authority.

There are a thousand little things in which the law of nature or education teaches us what is right and good, and which even earnest Christians do not hold themselves bound to obey. Now, remember, if you are unfaithful in that which is least, who will entrust you with the greater? Not God. If the voice of conscience tells you of some course of action that is the nobler or the better, and you choose another because it is easier or pleasing to self, you unfit yourself for the teaching of the Spirit by disobeying the voice of God in nature. A strong will always to do the right, to do the very best, as conscience points it out, is a will to do God's will. Paul writes, "I lie not, my conscience bearing me witness in the Holy Ghost." The Holy Ghost speaks through conscience: if you disobey and hurt conscience, you make it impossible for God to speak to you.

Obedience to God's will shows itself in tender regard for the voice of conscience. This holds good with regard to eating and drinking, sleeping and resting, spending money and seeking pleasure—let everything be brought into subjection to the will of God.

This leads to another thing of great importance in this connection. If you would live the life of true obedience, see that you maintain a good conscience before God, and never knowingly indulge in anything which is contrary to His mind. George Müller attributed all his happiness during seventy years to this, along with his love of God's Word. He had maintained a good conscience in all things, not continuing in a course he knew to be contrary to the will of God. Conscience is the guardian or monitor God has given you, to give warning when anything goes wrong. Up to the light you have, give heed to conscience. Ask God, by the teaching of His will, to give it more light. Seek the witness of conscience that you are acting up to that light. Conscience will become your encouragement and your helper, and give you the confidence, both that your obedience is accepted, and that your prayer for ever-increasing knowledge of the will is heard.

Even when the vow of unreserved obedience has been taken, there may still be two sorts of obedience—that of the law, and that of the gospel. Just as there are two Testaments, an Old and a New, so there are two styles of religion, two ways of serving

God. This is what Paul speaks of in Romans when he says, "Sin shall not have dominion over you: for ye are *not under law,* but under grace" (6: 14), and further speaks of our being "freed from the law," so "that we serve in newness of the spirit and *not in the oldness of the letter*" (7: 6); and then again reminds us, "Ye received *not again the spirit of bondage* unto fear, but ye received the Spirit of adoption" (8: 15).

The threefold contrast points very evidently to a danger existing among those Christians of still acting as if they were under the law, serving in the oldness of the letter and in the spirit of bondage. One great cause of the feebleness of so much Christian living is because it is more under law than under grace. Let us see what the difference is.

What the law demands from us, grace promises and performs for us.

The law deals with what we ought to do, whether we can or not, and by the appeal to motives of fear and love stirs us to do our utmost. But it gives no real strength, and so only leads to failure and condemnation. Grace points to what we cannot do, and offers to do it for us and in us.

The law comes with commands on stone or in a book. Grace comes in a living, gracious Person, who gives His presence and His power.

The law promises life, if we obey. Grace gives life, even the Holy Spirit, with the assurance that we can obey.

Human nature is ever prone to slip back out of grace into the law, and secretly to trust to trying and doing its utmost. The promises of grace are so divine, the gift of the Holy Spirit *to do all in us* is so wonderful, that few believe it. This is the reason they never dare take the vow of obedience, or, having taken it, turn back again. I beseech you, study well what gospel obedience is. The gospel is good tidings. Its obedience is part of that good tidings—*that grace, by the Holy Spirit, will do all in you.* Believe that, and let every undertaking to obey be in the joyous hopefulness that comes from faith in the exceeding abundance of grace, in the mighty indwelling of the Holy Spirit, in the blessed love of Jesus whose abiding presence makes obedience possible and certain.

This is one of the special and most beautiful aspects of gospel obedience. The grace which promises to work all through the Holy Spirit is the gift of eternal love. The Lord Jesus (who takes charge of our obedience, teaches it, and by His presence secures it to us) is He who loved us unto the death, who loves us with a love that passeth knowledge. Nothing can receive or know love but a loving heart. And it is this loving heart that enables us to obey. Obedience is the loving response to the divine love resting on us, and the only access to a fuller enjoyment of that love.

How our Lord insisted upon that in His farewell discourse! Thrice He repeats it in John 14:—*"If ye love me,* keep my commandments." "He that keepeth my commandments, he it is that *loveth me."* "If a man *love me,* he will keep my word." Is it not clear that love alone can give the obedience Jesus asks, and receive the blessing Jesus gives to obedience? The gift of the Spirit, the Father's love and His own, with the manifestation of Himself, the Father's love and His own making their abode with us, into these loving obedience gives the assured access.

In the next chapter He puts it from the other side, and shows how obedience leads to the enjoyment of God's love—He kept His Father's commandments, *and abides in His love.* If we keep His commandments, we shall *abide in His love.* He proved His love by giving His life for us; *we are His friends,* we shall enjoy His love, if we do what He commands us. Between His first love and our love in response to it, between our love and His fuller love in response to ours, *obedience is the one indispensable link.* True and full obedience is impossible, except as we live and love. "This is the love of God, that we keep his commandments."

Do beware of a legal obedience, striving after a life of true obedience under a sense of duty. Ask God to show you the "newness of life" which is needed for a new and full obedience. Claim the promise, "I will circumcise thine heart, to love the Lord thy God with all thy heart; and thou shalt obey the Lord thy God." Believe in the love of God and the grace of our Lord Jesus. Believe in the Spirit given in you, enabling you to love, and so causing you to walk in God's statutes. In the strength of this faith, in the assurance of sufficient grace, made perfect in weakness, enter into God's love and the life of living obedience it works. For it is nothing but the continual presence of Jesus in His love that can fit you for continual obedience.

I close with once again, and most urgently, pressing home this question. It lies at the very root of our life. The secret, half-unconscious thought that to live always well-pleasing to God is beyond our reach, eats away the very root of our strength. I beseech you to give a definite answer to the question.

If in the light of God's provision for obedience, of His promise of working all His good pleasure in you, of His giving you a new heart, with the indwelling of His Son and Spirit, you still fear obedience is not possible, do ask God to open your eyes truly to know His will. If your judgment be convinced, and you assent to the truth theoretically, and yet fear to give up yourself to such a life, I say to you, too, Do ask God to open your eyes and bring you to know *His will for yourself*. Do beware lest the secret fear of having to give up too much, of having to become too peculiar and entirely devoted to God, keep you back. Beware of seeking just religion enough to give ease to conscience, and then not desiring to do and be and give God all He is worthy of. And beware, above all, of "limiting" God, of making Him a liar, by refusing to believe what He has said He can and will do.

If our study in the school of obedience is to be of any profit, rest not till you have written it down— Daily obedience to all that God wills of me is possible, is possible to me. In His strength I yield myself to Him for it.

But remember, only on one condition. Not in the strength of your resolve or effort, but *that the unceasing presence of Christ and the unceasing teaching of the Spirit of all grace and power be your portion.* Christ, the obedient One, living in you, will secure your obedience. Obedience will be to you a life of love and joy in His fellowship.

We may be seeking for our growth in a more diligent use of the means of grace, and a more earnest striving to live in accordance with God's will, and yet entirely fail. The reason is, there is a secret root which must be removed. That root is the spirit of bondage, the legal spirit of self-effort, which hinders the humble faith that knows that God will work all, and yields to Him to do it.

In Christian Experience

THE HOUSE of Abraham was the Church of God of that age. The division in his house, one son, his own son, but born after the flesh, the other after the promise, was a divinely-ordained manifestation of the division there would be in all ages between the children of the bondwoman, those who served God in the spirit of bondage, and those who were children of the free and served Him in the Spirit of His Son. The passage teaches us what the whole Epistle confirms: that the Galatians had become entangled with a yoke of bondage, and were not standing fast in the freedom with which Christ makes free indeed. Instead of living in the New Covenant, in the Jerusalem which is from above, in the liberty which the Holy Spirit gives, their whole walk proved that, though Christians, they were of the Old Covenant, which bringeth forth children unto bondage. The passage teaches us the great truth, which it is of the utmost consequence for us to apprehend thoroughly, that a man, with a measure of the knowledge and experience of the grace of God, may prove, by a legal spirit, that he is yet practically, to a large extent, under the Old Covenant. And it will show us, with wonderful clearness, what the proofs are of the absence of the true New Covenant life.

A careful study of the Epistle shows us that the difference between the two Covenants is seen in three things. *The law and its works* are contrasted with the hearing of faith, *the flesh and its religion* with the flesh crucified, *the impotence to good* with a walk in the liberty and the power of the Spirit. May the Holy Spirit reveal to us this twofold life.

The first antithesis we find in Paul's words, "Received ye the Spirit by the works of the law, or the hearing of faith?" These Galatians had indeed been born into the New Covenant; they

161

had received the Holy Spirit. But they had been led away by Jewish teachers, and, though they had been justified by faith, they were seeking to be sanctified by works; they were looking for the maintenance and the growth of their Christian life to the observance of the law. They had not understood that, equally with the beginning, the progress of the Divine life is alone by faith, day by day receiving its strength from Christ alone; that in Jesus Christ nothing avails but faith working by love.

Almost every believer makes the same mistake as the Galatian Christians. Very few learn at conversion at once that it is only by faith that we stand, and walk, and live. They have no conception of the meaning of Paul's teaching about being dead to the law, freed from the law—about the freedom with which Christ makes us free. "As many as are led by the Spirit are not under the law." Regarding the law as a Divine ordinance for our direction, they consider themselves prepared and fitted by conversion to take up the fulfillment of the law as a natural duty. They know not that, in the New Covenant, the law written in the heart needs an unceasing faith in a Divine power, to enable us by a Divine power to keep it. They cannot understand that it is not to the law, but to a Living Person, that we are now bound, and that our obedience and holiness are possible only by the unceasing faith in His power ever working in us. It is only when this is seen that we are prepared truly to live in the New Covenant.

The second word, that reveals the Old Covenant spirit, is the word "flesh." Its contrast is, the flesh crucified. Paul asks: "Are ye so foolish? Having begun in the Spirit, are ye made perfect in the flesh?" Flesh means our sinful human nature. At his conversion the Christian has generally no conception of the terrible evil of his nature, and the subtlety with which it offers itself to take part in the service of God. It may be most willing and diligent in God's service for a time; it may devise numberless observances for making His worship pleasing and attractive; and yet this may be all only what Paul calls "making a fair show in the flesh," "glorying in the flesh," in man's will and man's efforts. This power of the religious flesh is one of the great marks of the Old Covenant religion; it misses the deep humility and spirituality of the true worship of God—a heart and life entirely dependent upon Him.

The proof that our religion is very much that of the religious flesh is that the sinful flesh will be found to flourish along with it. It was thus with the Galatians. While they were making a fair show in the flesh, and glorying in it, their daily life was full of bitterness and envy and hatred, and other sins. They were biting and devouring one another. Religious flesh and sinful flesh are one: no wonder that, with a great deal of religion, temper and selfishness and worldliness are so often found side by side. The religion of the flesh cannot conquer sin.

What a contrast to the religion of the New Covenant! What is the place the flesh has there? "They that are Christ's have *crucified the flesh,* with its desires and affections." Scripture speaks of the will of the flesh, the mind of the flesh, the lust of the flesh; all this the true believer has seen to be condemned and crucified in Christ: he has given it over to the death. He not only accepts the Cross, with its bearing of the curse, and its redemption from it, as his entrance into life; he glories in it as his only power day by day to overcome the flesh and the world. "I am crucified with Christ." "God forbid that I should glory save in the cross of my Lord Jesus Christ, by which I am crucified to the world." Even as nothing less than the death of Christ was needed to inaugurate the New Covenant, and the resurrection life that animates it, there is no entrance into the true New Covenant life other than by a partaking of that death.

"Fallen from grace." This is a third word that describes the condition of these Galatians in that bondage in which they were really impotent to all true good. Paul is not speaking of a final falling away here, for he still addresses them as Christians, but of their having wandered from that walk in the way of enabling and sanctifying grace, in which a Christian can get the victory over sin. So long as grace is principally connected with pardon and the entrance to the Christian life, the flesh is the only power in which to serve and work. But when we know what exceeding abundance of grace has been provided, and how God "makes all grace abound, that we may abound to all good works," we know that, as it is by faith, so too it is by grace alone that we stand a single moment or take a single step.

The contrast to this life of impotence and failure is found in the one word, "the Spirit." "If ye be led of the Spirit, ye are not under the law," with its demand on your own strength. "Walk in the Spirit, and ye shall not"—a definite, certain promise—"ye shall not fulfill the lusts of the flesh." The Spirit gives liberty from the law, from the flesh, from sin. "The fruit of the Spirit is love, peace, joy." Of the New Covenant promise, "I will put *my Spirit* within you, and *I will cause* you to walk in my statutes, and *ye shall keep* my judgments," the Spirit is the center and the sum. He is the power of the supernatural life of true obedience and holiness.

And what would have been the course that the Galatians would have taken if they had accepted this teaching of St. Paul? As they hear his question, "Now that ye have come to know God, how turn ye back again into the weak and beggarly rudiments, whereunto ye desire to be in bondage again?" they would have felt that there was but one course. Nothing else could help them but at once to turn back again to the path they had left. At the point where they had left it, they could enter again. With any one of them who wished to do so, this turning away from the Old Covenant legal spirit, and the renewed surrender to the Mediator of the New Covenant, could be the act of a moment— one single step. As the light of the New Covenant promise dawned upon him, and he saw how Christ was to be all, and faith all, and the Holy Spirit in the heart all, and the faithfulness of a Covenant-keeping God all in all, he would feel that he had but one thing to do—in utter impotence to yield himself to God, and in simple faith to count upon Him to perform what He had spoken. In Christian experience there may be still the Old Covenant life of bondage and failure. In Christian experience there may be a life that gives way entirely to the New Covenant grace and spirit. In Christian experience, when the true vision has been received of what the New Covenant means, a faith that rests fully on the Mediator of the New Covenant can enter at once into the life which the Covenant secures.

I cannot too earnestly beg all believers who long to know to the utmost what the grace of God can work in them, to study carefully the question whether the acknowledgment that our being in the bondage of the Old Covenant is the reason of our failure, and whether a clear insight into the possibility of an entire change in our relation to God is not what is needed to give us the help we seek. We may be seeking for our growth in a more diligent use of the means of grace, and a more earnest striving to live in accordance with God's will, and yet entirely fail. The reason is, there is a secret root of evil which must be removed. That root is the spirit of bondage, the legal spirit of self-effort, which hinders that humble faith that knows that God will work all, and yields to Him to do it. That spirit may be found amidst very great zeal for God's service, and very earnest prayer for His grace; it does not enjoy the rest of faith, and cannot overcome sin, because it does not stand in the liberty with which Christ has made us free, and does not know that where the Spirit of the Lord is, there is liberty. There the soul can say: "The law of the Spirit of life in Christ Jesus *hath made me free* from the law of sin and death." When once we admit heartily, not only that there are failings in our life, but that there is something radically wrong that can be changed, we shall turn with a new interest, with a deeper confession of ignorance and impotence, with a hope that looks to God alone for teaching and strength, to find that in the New Covenant there is an actual provision for every need.

The New Covenant is meant to meet the need for a power of not sinning, which the Old could not give.

The Everlasting Covenant

They shall be my people, and I will be their God. And I will make an everlasting covenant with them, that I will not turn away from them, to do them good; but I will put my fear in their hearts, that they shall not depart from me.

JEREMIAH 32: 38, 40.

A new heart also will I give you, and a new spirit will I put within you: and I will take the stony heart out of your flesh, and I will give you an heart of flesh. And I will put my spirit within you, and cause you to walk in my statutes, and ye shall keep my judgments, and do them. . . . Moreover, I will make a covenant of peace with them; it shall be an everlasting covenant with them.

EZEKIEL 36: 26, 27; 37: 26.

WE HAVE HAD the words of the institution of the New Covenant. Let us listen to the further teaching we have concerning it in Jeremiah and Ezekiel, where God speaks of it as an everlasting covenant. In every covenant there are two parties. And the very foundation of a covenant rests on the thought that each party is to be faithful to the part it has undertaken to perform. Unfaithfulness on either side breaks the covenant.

It was thus with the Old Covenant. God had said to Israel, *Obey my voice, and I will be your God* (Jer. 7: 23, 11: 4). These simple words contained the whole Covenant. And when Israel disobeyed, the Covenant was broken. The question of Israel being able or not able to obey was not taken into consideration: disobedience forfeited the privileges of the Covenant.

If a new covenant were to be made, and if that was to be better than the Old, this was the one thing to be provided for. No new covenant could be of any profit unless provision were made for securing obedience. Obedience there must be. God as Creator could never take His creatures into His favor and fellow-

167

ship except they obeyed Him. The thing would have been an impossibility. If the new covenant is to be better than the Old, if it is to be an everlasting covenant, never to be broken, it must make some sufficient provision for securing the obedience of the Covenant people.

And this is indeed the glory of the New Covenant, the glory that excelleth, that this provision has been made. In a way that no human thought could have devised, by a stipulation that never entered into any human covenant, by an undertaking in which God's infinite condescension and power and faithfulness are to be most wonderfully exhibited, by a supernatural mystery of Divine wisdom and grace, the New Covenant provides a guarantee, not only for God's faithfulness, *but for man's too!* And this in no other way than by God Himself undertaking to secure man's part as well as His own. Do try to get hold of this.

It is just because this, the essential part of the New Covenant, so exceeds and confounds all human thoughts of what a covenant means, that Christians, from the Galatians downward, have not been able to see and believe what the New Covenant really means. They have thought that human unfaithfulness was a factor permanently to be reckoned with as something utterly unconquerable and incurable, and that the possibility of a life of obedience, with the witness from within of a good conscience, and from above of God's pleasure, was not to be expected. They have therefore sought to stir the mind to its utmost by arguments and motives, and never realized how the Holy Spirit is to be the unceasing, universal, all-sufficient worker of everything that has to be wrought by the Christian.

Let us beseech God earnestly that He would reveal to us by the Holy Spirit the things that He hath prepared for them that love Him, things that have not entered into the heart of man, the wonderful life of the New Covenant. All depends upon our knowledge of what God will work in us. Listen to what God says in Jeremiah of the two parts of His everlasting Covenant, and in further elucidation of it. The central thought of that, *that the heart is to be put right,* is here reiterated and confirmed. "I will make an everlasting covenant with them, *that I will not turn away from* them, to do them good." That is, God will be unchangeably faithful. He will not turn from us. "But *I will put my fear into their heart, that they shall not depart from me.*" This is the second half: Israel will be unchangeably faithful too. And that because God will so put His fear in their heart that they shall not depart from Him. *As little as God will turn from them will they depart from Him!* As faithfully as He undertakes for the fulfillment of His part will He undertake for the fulfillment of their part, that they shall not depart from Him!

Listen to God's word in Ezekiel in regard to one of the terms of His Covenant of peace, His everlasting Covenant. (Ezek. 34: 25; 36: 27; 37: 26): "I will put my Spirit within you, and *cause you to walk in my statutes,* and *ye shall keep my judgments,* and do them." In the Old Covenant we have nothing of this sort. You have, on the contrary, from the story of the golden calf and the breaking of the Tables of the Covenant onward, the sad fact of continual departure from God. We find God longing for what He would so fain have seen, but was not to be found. "O that there were such an heart in them, that they would fear me, and keep all my commandments always" (Deut. 5: 29). We find throughout the Book of Deuteronomy, a thing without parallel in the history of any religion or religious lawgiver, that Moses most distinctly prophesies their forsaking of God, with the terrible curses and dispersion that would come upon them. It is only at the close of his threatenings (Deut. 30: 6, 8) that he gives the promise of the new time that would come: "The Lord thy God will circumcise thine heart, to love the Lord thy God with all thine heart, and with all thy soul, and *thou shalt obey* the voice of the Lord thy God." The whole Old Covenant was dependent on man's faithfulness: "The Lord thy God *keepeth covenant* with them *that keep* his commandments." God's keeping the Covenant availed little if man did not keep it. Nothing could help man until the "*if ye shall diligently keep*" of the law was replaced by the word of promise, "I will put my Spirit in you, and *ye shall keep* my judgments, and do them." The one supreme difference of the New Covenant, the one thing for which the Mediator, and the Blood, and the Spirit were given; the one fruit God sought and Himself engaged to bring forth was this: a heart filled with His fear and love, a heart to cleave unto Him and not depart from Him, a heart in which His Spirit and His law dwell, a heart that delights to do His will.

Here is the inmost secret of the New Covenant. It deals with the heart of man in a way of Divine power. It not only appeals to the heart by every motive of fear or love, of duty or gratitude. That the law also did. But it also reveals God Himself cleansing our heart and making it new, changing it entirely from a stony heart into a heart of flesh, a tender, living, loving heart, putting His Spirit within it, and so, by His Almighty Power and Love, breathing and working in it, making the promise true, *"I will cause you* to walk in my statutes, and *ye shall keep* my judgments."* A heart in perfect harmony with Himself, a life and walk in His way—God has engaged in a covenant to work this in us. He undertakes for our part in the Covenant as much as for His own.

This is nothing but the restoration of the original relation between God and the man He had made in His likeness. Man was on earth to be the very image of God, because God was to live and to work all in him, and he to find his glory and blessedness in thus owing all to God. This is the exceeding glory of the New Covenant, of the Pentecostal dispensation, that by the Holy Spirit God could now again be the indwelling life of His people, and so make the promise a reality: "I will cause you to walk in my statutes."

With God's presence secured to us every moment of the day —"I will not turn away from them"; with God's "fear put into our heart" by His own Spirit, and our heart thus responding to His holy presence; with our hearts thus made right with

God, we can, we shall walk in His statutes and keep his judgments.

The great sin of Israel under the Old Covenant, that by which they greatly grieved God, was this: "they limited the Holy One of Israel." Under the New Covenant there is not less danger of this sin. *It makes it impossible for God to fulfill His promises.* Let us seek, above everything, for the Holy Spirit's teaching to show us exactly what God has established the New Covenant for, that we may honor Him by believing all that His love has prepared for us.

And if we ask for the cause of the unbelief, that prevents the fulfillment of the promise, we shall find that it is not far to seek. It is, in most cases, the lack of desire for the promised blessing. In all who came to Jesus on earth the intensity of their desire for the healing they needed made them ready and glad to believe in His word. Where the law has done its full work, where the actual desire to be freed from every sin is strong, and masters the heart, the presence of the New Covenant, when once really understood, comes like bread to a famishing man. The subtle belief that it is impossible to be kept from sinning cuts away the power of accepting the promises of the everlasting Testament promise. God's Word, "I will put my fear in their heart, that *they shall not* depart from me"; "I will put my Spirit within you, and *ye shall* keep my judgment," is understood in some feeble sense, according to our experience, and not according to what the Word and what God means. And the soul settles down into a despair, or a self-contentment, that says it can never be otherwise, and makes true conviction for sin impossible.

Let me say to every reader who would fain be able to believe fully all that God says: Cherish every whisper of the conscience and of the Spirit that convinces of sin. Whatever it be, a hasty temper, a sharp word, an unloving or impatient thought, anything of selfishness or self-will—cherish that which condemns it in you as part of the schooling that is to bring you to Christ and the full possession of His salvation. The New Covenant is meant to meet the need for a power of not sinning, which the Old could not give. Come with that need; it will prepare and open the heart for all the everlasting Covenant secures you.

The life Christ lived in the Father is the life He imparts to us. . . .

Jesus the Mediator

I DO NOT KNOW that I can find a better case by which to illustrate the place Christ, the Mediator of the Covenant, takes in leading into its full blessing than that of the founder of the Keswick Convention, the late Canon Battersby.

It was at the Oxford Convention in 1873 that he witnessed to having "received a new and distinct blessing to which he had been a stranger before." For more than twenty-five years he had been most diligent as a minister of the gospel, and, as appears from his journals, most faithful in seeking to maintain a close walk with God. But he was ever disturbed by the consciousness of being overcome by sin. So far back as 1853 he had written, "I feel again how very far I am from enjoying habitually that peace and love and joy which Christ promises. I must confess that I have it not; and that very ungentle and unchristian tempers often strive within me for the master." When in 1873 he read what was being published of the Higher Life, the effect was to render him utterly dissatisfied with himself and his state. There were, indeed, difficulties he could not quite understand in that teaching, but he felt that he must either reach forward to better things, nothing less than redemption from *all* iniquities, or fall back more and more into worldliness and sin. At Oxford he heard an address on the rest of faith. It opened his eyes to the truth that a believer who really longs for deliverance from sinning must simply take Christ at His word, and reckon, without feeling, on Him to do His work of cleansing and keeping the soul. "I thought of the sufficiency of Jesus, and said, I *will* rest in Him, and I did rest in Him. I was afraid lest it should be a passing emotion; but I found that a presence of Jesus was graciously manifested to me in a way I knew not before, and that I *did abide in Him*. I do not

175

want to rest in these emotions, but just to believe, and to cling to Christ as my all." He was a man of very reserved nature, but felt it a duty ere the close of the Conference to confess publicly his past shortcoming, and testify openly to his having entered upon a new and definite experience.

In a paper written not long after this he pointed out what the steps are leading to this experience. *First,* a clear view of the possibilities of Christian attainment—a life in word and action, habitually governed by the Spirit, in constant communion with God, and continual victory over sin through abiding in Christ. *Then* the deliberate purpose of the will for a full renunciation of all the idols of the flesh or spirit, and a will-surrender to Christ. And then this last and important step: *We must look up to, and wait upon our ascended Lord for all that we need to enable us to do this.*

A careful perusal of this very brief statement will prove how everything centered here in Christ. The surrender for a life of continual communion and victory is to be to Christ. The strength for that life is to be in Him and from Him, by faith in Him. And *the power* to make the full surrender and rest in Him *was to be waited for* from *Him alone.*

In June, 1875, the first Keswick Convention was held. In the circular calling it, we read: "Many are everywhere thirsting that they may be brought to enjoy more of the Divine presence in their daily life, and a fuller manifestation of the Holy Spirit's power, whether in subduing the lusts of the flesh, or in enabling them to offer more effective service to God. It is certainly God's will that His children should be satisfied in regard to these long-ings, and there are those who can testify that He has satisfied them, and does satisfy them with daily fresh manifestations of His grace and power." The results of the very first Convention were most blessed, so that after its close he wrote: "There is a very remarkable resemblance in the testimonies I have since received as to the nature of the blessing obtained, viz., *the ability given* to make a full surrender to the Lord, and the consequent experience of an abiding peace, far exceeding anything previously experienced." Through all the chief thought was Christ, first drawing and enabling the soul to rest in Him, and then meeting it with the fulfillment of its desire, the abiding experience of His power to keep it in victory over sin and in communion with God.

And what was the fruit of this new experience? Eight years later Canon Battersby spoke: "It is now eight years since that I knew this blessing as my own. I cannot say that I have never for a moment ceased to trust the Lord to keep me. But I can say that so long as I have trusted Him, He has kept me; He has been faithful."

One would think that no words could make it plainer than the words of the Covenant state it—that the one difference between Old and New is that in the latter everything is to be done by God Himself. And yet believers and even teachers do not take it in. And even those who do, find it hard to live it out. Our whole being is so blinded to the true relation to God, His inconceivable Omnipresent Omnipotence working every moment in us is so far beyond the reach of human conception, that our little hearts cannot rise to the reality of His Infinite Love making itself one with us, and delighting to dwell in us, and to work all in us that has to be done there—that, when we think we have accepted the truth, we find it is only a thought. We are such strangers to the knowledge of what a God really is, as the actual life by which His creatures live. *In Him* we live and move and have our being. And especially is the knowledge of the Triune God too high for us, in that wonderful, most real, and most practical indwelling, to make which possible the Son became incarnate, and the Holy Spirit was sent forth into our hearts. Only they who confess their ignorance, and wait very humbly and persistently on our Blessed God to teach us by His Holy Spirit what that all-working indwelling is, can hope to have it revealed to them.

It is not long since I had occasion, in preparing a series of Bible Lessons for our Students Association, to make a study of the Gospel of St. John, and of the life of our Lord as set forth there. I cannot say how deeply I have been afresh impressed with that which I cannot but regard as the deepest secret of His life on earth, *His dependence on the Father*. It has come to me like a new revelation. Some twelve times and more He uses the word *not* and *nothing* of Himself. *Not* my will. *Not* my words. *Not* my honor. *Not* mine own glory. I can do *nothing* of myself. I speak *not* of myself. I came *not* of myself. I do *nothing* of myself.

Just think a moment what this means in connection with what He·tells us of His life in the Father. "As the Father hath life in himself; so hath he given to the Son to have life in himself" (5: 26). "That all men should honor the Son, even as they honor the Father" (5: 23). And yet this Son, who hath life in Himself even as the Father has, immediately adds (5: 30): "I can of mine own self do *nothing.*" We should have thought that with this life in Himself He would have the power of independent action as the Father has. But no. "The Son can do *nothing* of himself, but what he seeth the Father do." The chief mark of this Divine life He has in Himself is evidently unceasing dependence, receiving from the Father, by the moment, what He had to speak or do. *Nothing of myself* is manifestly as true of Him as it ever could be of the weakest or most sinful man. The life of the Father dwelling in Christ, and Christ in the Father, meant that just as truly as when He was begotten of the Father He received Divine life and glory from Him, so the continuation of that life came only by an eternal process of giving and receiving, as absolute as is the eternal generation itself. The more closely we study this truth and Christ's life in the light of it, the more we are compelled to say, the deepest root of Christ's relationship to the Father, the true reason why He was so well-pleasing, the secret of His glorifying the Father, was this: *He allowed God to do all in Him*. He received and wrought out only what God wrought in Him. His whole attitude was that of the open ear, the servant spirit, the childlike dependence that waited for all on God.

The infinite importance of this truth in the Christian life is easily felt. The life Christ lived in the Father is the life He imparts to us. We are to abide in Him and He in us, *even as* He in the Father and the Father in Him. And if the secret of His abiding in the Father be this unceasing self-abnegation—"I can do nothing of myself"—this life of most entire and absolute dependence and waiting upon God, must it not be far more the most marked feature of our Christian life, the first and all-pervading disposition we seek to maintain? In a little book of William Law's, he especially insists upon this in his so striking repetition of the call, if we would die to self in order to have the birth of Divine love in our souls, to sink down in humility, meekness, patience, and resignation to God. I think that no one who at all enters into this advice but will feel what new point is given to it by the remembrance of how this entire self-renunciation was not only one of the many virtues in the character of Christ, but, indeed, that first essential one without which God could have wrought nothing in Him, through which God did work all.

Let us make Christ's words our own: *"I can do nothing of myself."* Take it as the keynote of a single day. Look up and see the Infinite God waiting to do everything as soon as we are ready to give up all to Him and to receive all from Him. Bow down in lowly worship, and wait for the Holy Spirit to work some measure of the mind of Christ in you. Do not be disconcerted if you do not learn the lesson at once: there is the God of love waiting to do everything in him who is willing to be nothing. At moments the teaching appears dangerous, at other times terribly difficult. The Blessed Son of God teaches it us—this was His whole life: I can do nothing of myself. He is our life; He will work it in us. And when as the Lamb of God He begets this His disposition in us, we shall be prepared for Him to rise on us and shine in us in His heavenly glory.

"Nothing of myself"—that word spoken eighteen hundred years ago, coming out of the inmost depths of the heart of the Son of God—is a seed in which the power of the eternal life is hidden. Take it straight from the heart of Christ and hide it in your heart. Meditate on it till it reveals the beauty of His Divine meekness and humility, and explains how all the power and glory of God could work in Him. Believe in it as containing the very life and disposition which you need, and believe in Christ, whose Spirit dwells in the seed to make it true in you. Begin, in single acts of self-emptying, to offer it to God as the one desire of your heart. Count upon God accepting them, and meeting them with His grace, to make the acts into habits, and the habits into dispositions. And you may depend upon it, there is nothing that will lift you so near to God, nothing that will unite you closer to Christ, nothing that will prepare you for the abiding presence and power of God working in you, as the death to self which is found in the simple word—*nothing of myself.*

This word is one of the keys to the New Covenant Life. As I believe that God is actually to work all in me, I shall see that the one thing that is hindering me is my doing something of myself. As I am willing to learn from Christ by the Holy Spirit to say truly, *Nothing of myself,* I shall have the true preparation to receive all God has engaged to work, and the power confidently to expect it. I shall learn that the whole secret of the New Covenant is just one thing: *God works all!* The seal of the Covenant stands sure: "I the Lord have spoken it, and I *will do it.*"

His humility was simply the surrender of Himself to God, to allow God to do in Him what He pleased, whatever men around might say of Him, or do to Him.

The Humility of Jesus

Learn of me; for I am meek and lowly in heart.
MATTHEW 11: 29.

Whosoever will be chief among you, let him be your servant, even as the Son of man came to minister.
MATTHEW 20: 27, 28.

IN THE GOSPEL of John we have the inner life of our Lord laid open to us. Jesus speaks frequently of His relation to the Father, of the motives by which He is guided, of His consciousness of the power and spirit in which He acts. Though the word "humble" does not occur, we shall nowhere in Scripture see so clearly wherein His humility consisted. We have already said that this grace is in truth nothing but that simple consent of the creature to let God be all, in virtue of which it surrenders itself to His working alone. In Jesus we shall see how both as the Son of God in heaven, and as man upon earth, He took the place of entire subordination, and gave God the honor and the glory which are due to Him. And what He taught so often was made true to Himself: "He that humbleth himself shall be exalted." As it is written, "He humbled himself, therefore God highly exalted him."

Listen to the words in which our Lord speaks of His relation to the Father, and see how unceasingly He uses the words *not*, and *nothing*, of Himself. The *not I*, in which Paul expresses his relation to Christ, is the very spirit of what Christ says of His relation to the Father.

"The Son can do nothing of himself" (John 5: 19).

"I can of my own self do *nothing;* my judgment is just, because I seek *not* mine own will" (John 5: 30).

"I receive *not* glory from men" (John 5: 41).

183

"I am come *not* to do mine own will" (John 6: 38).

"My teaching is *not* mine" (John 7: 16).

"I am *not* come of myself" (John 7: 28).

"I do *nothing* of myself" (John 8: 28).

"I have *not* come of myself, but he sent me" (John 8: 42).

"I seek *not* mine own glory" (John 8: 50).

"The words that I say I speak *not* from myself" (John 14: 10).

"The word which ye hear is *not* mine" (John 14: 24).

These words open to us the deepest roots of Christ's life and work. They tell us how it was that the Almighty God was able to work His mighty redemption work through Him. They show what Christ counted the state of heart which became Him as the Son of the Father. They teach us what the essential nature and life is of that redemption which Christ accomplished and now communicates. It is this: He was nothing, that God might be all. He resigned Himself with His will and His powers entirely for the Father to work in Him. Of His own power, His own will, and His own glory, of His whole mission with all His works and His teaching—of all this He said, It is not I; I am nothing; I have given myself to the Father to work; I am nothing, the Father is all.

This life of entire self-abnegation, of absolute submission and dependence upon the Father's will, Christ found to be one of perfect peace and joy. He lost nothing by giving all to God. God honored His trust, and did all for Him, and then exalted Him to His own right hand in glory. And because Christ had thus humbled Himself before God, and God was ever before Him, He found it possible to humble Himself before men too, and to be the Servant of all. His humility was simply the surrender of Himself to God, to allow God to do in Him what He pleased, whatever men around might say of Him, or do to Him.

It is in this state of mind, in this spirit and disposition, that the redemption of Christ has its virtue and efficacy. It is to bring us to this disposition that we are made partakers of Christ. This is the true self-denial to which our Saviour calls us, the acknowledgment that self has nothing good in it, except as an empty vessel which God must fill, and that its claim to be or do anything may not for a moment be allowed. It is in this, above and before everything, in which the conformity to Jesus consists, the being and doing nothing of ourselves, that God may be all.

Here we have the root and nature of true humility. It is because this is not understood or sought after that our humility is so superficial and so feeble. We must learn of Jesus, how He is meek and lowly of heart. He teaches us where true humility takes its rise and finds its strength—in the knowledge that it is God who worketh all in all, that our place is to yield to Him in perfect resignation and dependence, in full consent to be and to do nothing of ourselves. This is the life Christ came to reveal and to impart—a life to God that came through death to sin and self. If we feel that this life is too high for us and beyond our reach, it must but the more urge us to seek it in Him; it is the indwelling Christ who will live in us this life, meek and lowly. If we long for this let us, meantime, above everything, seek the holy secret of the knowledge of the nature of God as He every moment works all in all; the secret, of which all nature and every creature, and above all, every child of God, is to be the witness, that it is nothing but a vessel, a channel, through which the living God can manifest the riches of His wisdom, power, and goodness. The root of all virtue and grace, of all faith and acceptable worship, is that we know that we have nothing but what we receive, and bow in deepest humility to wait upon God for it.

It was because this humility was not only a temporary sentiment, wakened up and brought into exercise when He thought of God, but the very spirit of His whole life, that Jesus was just as humble in His intercourse with men as with God. He felt Himself the Servant of God for the men whom God made and loved; as a natural consequence, He counted Himself the Servant of men, that through Him God might do His work of love.

He never for a moment thought of seeking His own honor, or asserting His own power to vindicate Himself. His whole spirit was that of a life yielded to God to work in. It is not until Christians study the humility of Jesus as the very essence of His redemption, as the very blessedness of the life of the Son of God, as the only true relation to the Father, and therefore as that which Jesus must give us if we are to have any part with Him, that the terrible lack of actual, heavenly, manifest humility will become a burden and a sorrow, and our ordinary religion be set aside to secure this, the first and the chief of the marks of the Christ within us.

Are you clothed with humility? Ask your daily life. Ask Jesus. Ask your friends. Ask the world. And begin to praise God that there is opened up to you in Jesus a heavenly humility of which you have hardly known, and through which a heavenly blessedness you possibly have never yet tasted can come in to you.

He can reveal Himself. I cannot reveal Him unto you; you cannot grasp Him; but He can shine into your heart. How can I see the sunlight tomorrow morning? . . . The sunlight will reveal itself. How can I know Christ? Christ can reveal Himself.

The Presence of Christ

*But straightway Jesus spake unto them, saying, Be of good cheer;
it is I; be not afraid.*

MATTHEW 14: 27.

ALL WE HAVE HAD about the work of the blessed Spirit is dependent upon what we think of Jesus, for it is *from* Christ Jesus
that the Spirit comes to us; it is *to* Christ Jesus that the Spirit
ever brings us; and the one need of the Christian life day by day
and hour by hour is this, the presence of the Son of God. God is
our salvation. If I have Christ with me and Christ in me, I have
full salvation. We have spoken about the life of failure and of
the flesh, about the life of unbelief and disobedience, about the
life of ups and downs, the wilderness life of sadness and of sorrow; but we have heard, and we have believed, there is deliverance. Bless God, He brought us out of Egypt, that He might
bring us into Canaan, into the very rest of God and Jesus Christ.
He is our peace, He is our rest. Oh, if I may only have the
presence of Jesus as the victory over every sin, the presence of
Jesus as the strength for every duty, then my life shall be in the
full sunshine of God's unbroken fellowship, and the word will
be fulfilled to me in most blessed experience, "Son, thou art ever
with me, and all I have is thine," and my heart shall answer,
"Father, I never knew it, but it is true, I am ever with thee and
all Thou hast is mine." God has given all He has to Christ, and
God longs that Christ should have you and me entirely. I come
to every hungry heart and say, "If you want to live to the glory
of God, seek one thing, to claim, to believe that the presence
of Jesus can be with you every moment of your life.

I want to speak about the presence of Jesus as it is set before

189

us in that blessed story of Christ's walking on the sea. Come and look with me at some points that are suggested to us.

1. Think, first, of the presence of Christ *lost*. You know the disciples loved Christ, clung to Him, and with all their failings they delighted in Him. But what happened? The Master went up into the mountain to pray, and sent them across the sea all alone without Him; there came a storm, and they toiled, rowed, and labored, but the wind was against them, they made no progress, they were in danger of perishing, and how their hearts said, "Oh, if only the Master were here!" But His presence was gone. They missed Him. Once before, they had been in a storm, and Christ had said, "Peace, be still," and all was well; but here they are in darkness, danger, and terrible trouble, and no Christ to help them. Ah, isn't that the life of many a believer at times? I get into darkness, I have committed sin, the cloud is on me, I miss the face of Jesus; and for days and days I work, worry, and labor; but it is all in vain, for I miss the presence of Christ. Oh, beloved, let us write that down—the presence of Jesus lost is the cause of all our wretchedness and failure.

2. Look at the second step—the presence of Jesus *dreaded*. They were longing for the presence of Christ, and Christ came after midnight: He came walking on the water amid the waves; but they didn't recognize Him, and they cried out for fear, "It is a spirit!" Their beloved Lord was coming nigh, and they knew Him not. They dreaded His approach. And, ah, how often have I seen a believer dreading the approach of Christ, crying out for Him, longing for Him, and yet dreading His coming. And why? Because Christ came in a fashion that they expected not.

Perhaps some have been saying, "Alas, alas I fear I never can have the abiding presence of Christ!" You have heard what we have said about a life in the Spirit: you have heard what we have said about abiding ever in the presence of God and in His fellowship, and you have been afraid of it, afraid of it; and you have said, "It is too high and too difficult." You have dreaded the very teaching that was going to help you. Jesus came to you in the teaching, and you didn't recognize His love.

Or, perhaps, He came in a way that you dreaded His presence. Perhaps God has been speaking to you about some sin. There is that sin of temper, or that sin of unlovingness, or that sin of unforgivingness, or that sin of worldliness, compromise, and fellowship with the world; that love of man and man's honor, that fear of man and man's opinion, or that pride and self-confidence. God has been speaking to you about it, and yet you have been frightened. That was Jesus wanting to draw you nigh, but you were afraid. You don't see how you can give up all that; you are not ready to say, "At any sacrifice I am going to have that taken out of me, and I *will* give it up," and while God and Christ were coming nigh to bless you, you were afraid of Him.

Oh, believers, at other times Christ has come to you with affliction, and perhaps you have said, "If I want to be entirely holy, I know I shall have to be afflicted, and I am afraid of affliction," and you have dreaded the thought, "Christ may come to me in affliction." The presence of Christ dreaded!—oh, beloved, I want to tell you it is all misconception. The disciples had no reason to dread that "spirit" coming there, for it was Christ Himself; and when God's word comes close to you and touches your heart, remember that is Christ out of whose mouth goes the two-edged sword. It is Christ in His love coming to cut away the sin, that He may fill your heart with the blessing of God's love. Beware of dreading the presence of Christ.

3. Then comes the third thought—the presence of Christ *revealed*. Bless God! When Christ heard how they cried, He spoke the words of the text, "Be of good cheer; it is I; be not afraid." Ah, what gladness those words brought to those hearts! There is Jesus; that dark object appears—that dreaded form. It is our blessed Lord Himself. And, dear friends, the Master's object, whether it be by affliction or otherwise, is to prepare for receiving

the presence of Christ, and through it all Jesus speaks, "It is I; be not afraid." The presence of Christ revealed! I want to tell you that the Son of God, oh, believer, is longing to reveal Himself to you. Listen! *Listen!* LISTEN! Is there any longing heart? Jesus says, "Be of good cheer; it is I; be not afraid."

Oh, beloved, God has given us Christ. And does God want me to have Christ every moment? Without doubt. God wants the presence of Christ to be the joy of every hour of my life; and, if there is one thing sure, Christ can reveal Himself to me every moment. Are you willing to come and claim this privilege? He can reveal Himself. I cannot reveal Him to you; you cannot grasp Him; but He can shine into your heart. How can I see the sunlight tomorrow morning if I am spared? The sunlight will reveal itself. How can I know Christ? Christ can reveal Himself. And, ere I go further, I pray you to set your heart upon this, and to offer the humble prayer, "Lord, now reveal Thyself to me so that I may never lose the sight of Thee. Give me to understand that through the thick darkness Thou comest to make Thyself known." Let not one heart doubt, however dark it may be—at midnight, whatever midnight there be in the soul—at midnight, in the dark, Christ can reveal Himself. Ah, thank God, often after a life of ten and twenty years of dawn, after a life of ten and twenty years of struggling, now in the light, and now in the dark, there comes a time when Jesus is willing just to give Himself to us, nevermore to part. God grant us that presence of Jesus!

4. And now comes the fourth thought. The presence of Jesus *lost* was the first; the presence of Jesus *dreaded* was the second; the presence of Jesus *revealed* was the third; the presence of Jesus *desired* is the fourth. What happened? Peter heard the Lord, and he was content. He was in the boat, and yonder was Jesus, some thirty, forty, fifty yards distant, and He made as though He would have passed them; and Peter—showing what terrible failure and carnality there was in him; but, bless the Lord, Peter's heart was right with Christ, and he wanted to claim His presence —Peter said, "Lord, if it be thou, bid me come upon the water to

thee." Yes, Peter could not rest; he wanted to be as near to Christ as possible. He saw Christ walking on the water; he remembered Christ had said, "Follow me"; he remembered how Christ, with the miraculous draught of fishes, had proved that He was Master of the sea, and he remembered how Christ had stilled the storm; and, without argument or reflection, all at once he said, "There is my Lord manifesting himself in a new way; there is my Lord exercising a new and supernatural power, and I can go to my Lord; he is able to make me walk where he walks." He wanted to walk like Christ, he wanted to walk near Christ. He didn't say, "Lord, let me walk around the sea here," but said, "Lord, let me come to thee."

Friends, would you not like to have the presence of Christ in this way? Not that Christ should come down; that is what many Christians want; they want to continue in their sinful walk, they want to continue in their worldly walk, they want to continue in their old life, and they want Christ to come down to them with His comfort, His presence, and His love; but that cannot be. If I am to have the presence of Christ I must walk as He walked. His walk was a supernatural one. He walked in the love and in the power of God. Most people walk according to the circumstances in which they are, and most people say, "I am depending upon circumstances for my religion." A hundred times over you hear people say, "My circumstances prevent my enjoying unbroken fellowship with Jesus." What were the circumstances that were round about Christ? The wind and the waves—and Christ walked triumphant over circumstances; and Peter said, "Like my Lord I can triumph over all circumstances: anything around me is nothing if I have Jesus." He longed for the presence of Christ. Would God that, as we look at the life of Christ upon earth, as we look how Christ walked and conquered the waves, every one of us could say, "I want to walk like Jesus." If that is your heart's desire you can expect the presence of Jesus; but so long as you want to walk on a lower level than Christ, so long as you want to have a little of the world, and a little of self-will, do not expect to have the presence of Christ. Near Christ, and like Christ —the two things go together. Have you taken that in? Peter wanted to walk like Christ that he might get near Christ, and it is this I want to offer every one of you. I want to say to the weakest believer, "With God's presence you can have the presence and fellowship of Christ all the day long, your whole life through." I want to bring you that promise, but I must give God's condition—walk like Christ, and you shall always abide near Christ. The presence of Christ invites you to come and have unbroken fellowship with Him.

5. Then comes the next thought. We have just had the presence of Christ desired, and my next thought is the presence of Christ *trusted*. The Lord Jesus said, "Come," and what did Peter do? He stepped out of the boat. How did he dare to do it against all the laws of nature? How did he dare to do it? He sought Christ, he heard Christ's voice, he trusted Christ's presence and power, and in the faith of Christ he said, "I can walk on the water," and he stepped out of the boat. Here is the turning point; here is the crisis. Peter saw Christ in the manifestation of a supernatural power, and Peter believed that supernatural power could work in him, and he could live a supernatural life. He believed this applied to walking on the sea, and herein lies the whole secret of the life of faith. Christ had supernatural power—the power of heaven, the power of holiness, the power of fellowship with God—and Christ can give me grace to live as He lived. If I will, but, like Peter, look at Christ and say to Christ, "Lord, speak the word, and I will come," and if I will listen to Christ saying, "Come," I, too, shall have power to walk upon the waves.

Have you ever seen a more beautiful and more instructive symbol of the Christian life? I once preached on it many years ago, and the thought that filled my heart then was this, the Christian life compared with Peter walking on the waves: nothing so difficult and impossible without Christ, nothing so blessed and safe with Christ. That is the Christian life—impossible without Christ's nearness, most safe and blessed, however difficult, if I only have the presence of Christ. Believers, we have tried to call you to a better life, to a spiritual life, to a holy life, a life in the Spirit, to a life in the fellowship with God. There is only one thing can enable you to live it—you must have the Lord Jesus hold your hand every minute of the day. "But can that be?" you ask. Yes, it can be. "I have so much to think of. Sometimes for four or five hours of the day I have to go into the very thick of business and have some ten men standing around me, each claiming my attention. How can I, how can I always have the presence of Jesus?" Beloved, because Jesus is your God and loves you wonderfully, and is able to make His presence more clear to you than that of ten men who are standing around you. If you will in the morning take time and enter into your covenant every morning with Him, "My Lord Jesus, nothing can satisfy me but Thy abiding presence," He will give it to you, He will surely give it to you. Oh, Peter trusted the presence of Christ, and he said, "If Christ calls me I can walk on the waves to him." Shall we trust the presence of Christ? To walk through all the circumstances and temptations of life is exactly like walking on the water. You do not know how strong the temptations of Satan may come; but do believe God wants you to walk in a supernatural life above human power. God wants you to live a life in Christ Jesus. Do you want to live that life? Come, then, and say, "Jesus, I have heard Thy promise that Thy presence will go with me. Thou hast said, My presence shall go with thee, and, Lord, I claim it; I trust Thee."

6. Now, the sixth step in this wonderful history. The presence of Christ *forgotten*. Peter got out of the boat and began to walk toward the Lord Jesus with his eye fixed upon Him. The presence of Christ was trusted by him, and he walked boldly over the waves; but all at once he took his eye off Jesus, and he began at once to sink, and there was Peter, his walk of faith at an end, all drenched and drowning and crying, "Lord, help me!" There are some of you saying in your hearts, I know, "Ah, that's what will come of your higher-life Christians." There are people who

say, "You never can live that life; do not talk of it; you must always be failing." Peter always failed before Pentecost. It was because the Holy Spirit had not yet come, and therefore his experience goes to teach us that while Peter was still in the life of the flesh he must fail, somehow or other. But, thank God, there was One to lift him out of the failure, and our last point will be to prove that out of that failure he came into closer union with Jesus than ever before, and into deeper dependence. But listen, first, while I speak to you about this failure.

Someone may say, "I have been trying to say, 'Lord, I will live it'; but tell me, suppose failure comes, what then?" Learn from Peter what you ought to do. What did Peter do? The very opposite of what most do. What did he do when he began to sink? That very moment, without one word of self-reproach or self-condemnation, he cried, "Lord, help me!" I wish I could teach every Christian that. I remember the time in my spiritual life when that became clear to me; for up to that time, when I failed, my only thought was to reproach and condemn myself, and I thought that would do me good. I found it didn't do me good, and I learn from Peter that, the very moment I fail, my work is to say, "Jesus, Master, help me!" And the very moment I say that, Jesus does help me. Remember, failure is not an impossibility. I can conceive more than one Christian who said, "Lord, I claim the fullness of the Holy Ghost. I want to live every hour of every day filled with the Holy Spirit"; and I can conceive that an honest soul who said that with a trembling faith, yet may have fallen—I want to say to that soul, Don't be discouraged. If failure comes, at once, without any waiting, appeal to Jesus. He is always ready to hear, and the very moment you find there is the temper, the hasty word, or some other wrong, at once the living Jesus is near, so gracious, and so mighty. Appeal to Him and there will be help at once. If you will learn to do this, Jesus will lift you up and lead you on to a walk where His strength will secure you from failure.

7. And then comes my last thought. The presence of Jesus

was forgotten while Peter looked at the waves; but now, finally, we have the presence of Jesus *restored*. Yes, Christ stretched out His hand to save Peter. Possibly—for Peter was a very proud, self-confident man—possibly he had to sink there to teach him that it was not his faith that could save him, but the power of Christ. God wants us to learn the lesson that when we fall, then we can cry to Jesus, and at once He reaches out His hand. Remember, Peter walked back to the boat without sinking again. Why? Because Christ was very near him. Remember, it is quite possible, if you use your failure rightly, to be far nearer Christ after it than before. Use it rightly, I say. That is, come and acknowledge, "In me there is nothing, but I am going to trust my Lord unboundedly." Let every failure teach you to cling afresh to Christ, and He will prove Himself a mighty and a loving Helper. The presence of Jesus restored! Yes, Christ took Peter by the hand and helped him, and I don't know whether they walked hand in hand those forty or fifty yards back to the boat, or whether Christ allowed Peter to walk beside Him; but this I know, they were very near to each other, and it was the nearness to his Lord that strengthened Peter.

Remember what has taken place since that happened to Peter. The cross has been erected, the blood has been shed, the grave has been opened, the resurrection has been accomplished, heaven has been opened, and the Spirit of the Exalted One has come down. Do believe that it is possible for the presence of Jesus to be with us every day and all the way. Your God has given you Christ, and He wants to give you Christ into your heart in such a way that His presence will be with you every moment of your life.

Who is willing to lift up his eyes and his heart and to exclaim, "I want to live according to God's standard"? Who is willing? Who is willing to cast himself into the arms of Jesus and to live a life of faith victorious over the winds and the waves, over the circumstances and difficulties? Who is willing to say this, "Lord, bid me come to Thee upon the water"? Are you willing?

Listen! Jesus says, "Come." Will you step out at this moment? Yonder is the boat, the old life that Peter had been leading; he had been familiar with the sea from his boyhood, and that boat was a very sacred place; Christ had sat beside him there; Christ had preached from that boat; from that boat of Peter's Christ had given the wonderful draught of fishes. It was a very sacred boat, but Peter left it to come to a place more sacred still—walking with Jesus on the water, a new and a Divine experience. Your Christian life may be a very sacred thing; you may say, "Christ saved me by His blood, He has given me many an experience of grace; God has proved His grace in my heart." But you confess, "I haven't got the real life of abiding fellowship; the winds and the waves often terrify me, and I sink." Oh, come out of the boat of past experiences at once; come out of the boat of external circumstances; come out of the boat, and step out on the word of Christ, and believe, "With Jesus I can walk upon the water." When Peter was in the boat, what had he between him and the bottom of the sea? A couple of planks, but when he stepped out upon the water what had he between him and the sea? Not a plank, but the word of the Almighty Jesus. Will you come, and without any experience, will you rest upon the word of Jesus, "Lo, I am with you alway"? Will you rest upon His word, "Be of good cheer; fear not; it is I"? Every moment Jesus lives in heaven, every moment by His Spirit Jesus whispers that word, and every moment He lives to make it true. Accept it now, accept it now! My Lord Jesus is equal to every emergency. My Lord Jesus can meet the wants of every soul. My whole heart says, "He *can*, He *can* do it; He *will*, He *will* do it!" Oh, come believers, and let us claim most deliberately, most quietly, most restfully—let us claim, claim it, *claim it*, CLAIM IT.

A readiness to believe every promise implicitly, to obey every command unhesitatingly, to "stand perfect and complete in all the will of God," is the only true spirit of Bible study.

Meditation

*Blessed is the man whose delight is in the law of the Lord; and
in his law doth he meditate day and night.*
>   PSALM 1: 1, 2. (JOSHUA 1: 8; PSALM 119: 15, 23, 48,
>   78, 97, 99 and 148; I TIMOTHY 5: 15).

*Let the words of my mouth, and the meditation of my heart, be
acceptable in thy sight, O Lord.*
>   PSALMS 19: 14 and 49: 3.

THE TRUE AIM of education, study, reading, is to be found, not
in what is brought into us, but in what is brought out of ourselves, by the awakening into active exercise of our inward
power. This is as true of the study of the Bible as of any other
study. God's Word works its true blessing only when the truth
it brings to us has stirred the inner life, and reproduced itself in
resolve, trust, love, or adoration. When the heart has received the
Word through the mind, and has had its spiritual powers called
out and exercised on it, the Word is no longer void, but has done
that whereunto God has sent it. It has become part of our life,
and strengthened us for new purpose and effort.

It is in meditation that the heart holds and appropriates the
Word. Just as in reflection the understanding grasps all the meaning and bearings of a truth, so in meditation the heart assimilates
it and makes it a part of its own life. We need continual remind-
ing that the heart means the will and the affection. The meditation of the heart implies desire, acceptance, surrender, love. Out
of the heart are the issues of life; what the heart truly believes,
that it receives with love and joy, and allows to master and rule
the life. The intellect gathers and prepares the food on which we
are to feed. In meditation the heart takes it in and feeds on it.

201

The art of meditation needs to be cultivated. Just as a man needs to be trained to concentrate his mental powers so as to think clearly and accurately, so a Christian needs carefully to consider and meditate, until the holy habit has been formed of yielding up the whole heart to every word of God.

Sometimes it is asked how this power of meditation can be cultivated. The very first thing is to present ourselves before God. It is His Word; that Word has no power of blessing apart from Him. It is into His presence and fellowship that the Word is meant to bring us. Practice His presence, and take the Word as from Himself in the assurance that He will make it work effectually in the heart. In Psalm 119 you have the word seven times, but each time as part of a prayer addressed to God. "I will meditate in *thy* precepts." "Thy servant did meditate in *thy* statutes." "O how I love *thy* law, it is my meditation all the day." Meditation is the heart turning towards God with His own Word, seeking to take it up into the affection and will, into its very life.

Another element of true meditation is quiet restfulness. In our study of Scripture, in our endeavor to grasp an argument, or to master a difficulty, our intellect often needs to put forth its utmost efforts. The habit of soul required in meditation is different. Here we turn with some truth we have found, or some mystery in which we are waiting for divine teaching to hide the word we are engaged with in the depth of the heart, and believe that, by the Holy Spirit, its meaning and power will be revealed in our inner life. "Thou desirest truth in the inward parts; and in the hidden part thou shalt make me to know wisdom." In the description of our Lord's mother we are told: "Mary kept all these things and pondered them in her heart." In His mother keeping all these sayings in her heart we have the image of a soul that has begun to know Christ and is on the sure way to know Him better.

It is hardly necessary to say further that in meditation the personal application takes a prominent place. This is all too little the case with our intellectual study of the Bible. Its object is to know and understand. In meditation the chief object is to appropriate and experience. A readiness to believe every promise implicitly, to obey every command unhesitatingly, to "stand perfect and complete in all the will of God," is the only true spirit of Bible study. It is in quiet meditation that this faith is exercised, that this allegiance is rendered, that the full surrender to all God's will is made, and that assurance is received of grace to perform our vows.

And then meditation must lead to prayer. It provides matter for prayer. It must lead on to prayer, to ask and receive definitely what it has seen in the Word or accepted in the Word. Its value is that it is the preparation for prayer, deliberate and wholehearted supplication for what the heart has felt that the Word has revealed as needful or possible. That means the rest of faith, that looks upward in the assurance that the Word will open up and prove its power in the soul that meekly and patiently gives itself away to it.

The reward of resting for a time from intellectual effort, and cultivating the habit of holy meditation, will be that in course of time the two will be brought into harmony, and all our study be animated by the spirit of a quiet waiting on God and a yielding up of the heart and life to the Word.

Our fellowship with God is meant for all the day. The blessing of securing a habit of true meditation in the morning watch will be that we shall be brought nearer the blessedness of the man of the first Psalm; "Blessed is the man whose delight is in the law of the Lord; and in his law doth he meditate day and night."

Let all workers and leaders of God's people remember that they need this more than others if they are to train them to it, and keep up their own communication unbroken with the only source of strength and blessing. God says, "I will be with thee; I will not fail nor forsake thee. Only be thou strong and very courageous that thou mayest observe to do according to all the law . . . that thou mayest prosper whithersoever thou goest. This book of the law shall not depart out of thy mouth; *thou shalt meditate therein day and night.* . . . Then thou shalt have good success. . . . Be strong and of a good courage."

"Let the words of my mouth, and the meditation of my heart, be acceptable in *thy sight,* O Lord, my strength, and my redeemer." Let nothing less be your aim—that your meditation may be acceptable in His sight—part of the spiritual sacrifice you offer. Let nothing less be your prayer and expectation, that your meditation may be true worship, the living surrender of the heart to God's Word in His presence.

Christ's Church and the world are sufferers today, oh, so terribly, not only because so many of its members are not working for God, but because so much working for God is done without waiting on God.

Waiting and Working

They that wait upon the Lord shall renew their strength. . . .
*Neither hath the eye seen, O God, besides thee, who worketh for
him that* waiteth for him.

ISAIAH 40: 31; 64: 4.

H ERE WE HAVE two texts in which the connection between waiting and working is made clear. In the first we see that waiting
brings the needed strength for working—that it fits for joyful
and unwearied work. "They that wait upon the Lord shall renew
their strength; they shall mount up on eagles' wings; they shall
run, and not be weary; they shall walk, and not faint." Waiting
on God has its value in this: it makes us strong in work for God.
The second reveals the secret of this strength. "God worketh for
him that waiteth for him." The waiting on God secures the
working of God for us and in us, out of which our work must
spring. The two passages teach the great lesson, that as waiting
on God lies at the root of all true working for God, so working
for God must be the fruit of all true waiting on Him. Our great
need is to hold the two sides of the truth in perfect conjunction
and harmony.

There are some who say they wait upon God, but who do
not work for Him. For this there may be various reasons. Here
is one who confounds true waiting on God (in living, direct
intercourse with Him as the Living One), and the devotion to
Him of the energy of the whole being, with the slothful, helpless
waiting that excuses itself from all work until God, by some special impulse, has made work easy. Here is another who waits on
God more truly, regarding it as one of the highest exercises of the
Christian life, and yet has never understood that at the root of all

207

true waiting there must lie the surrender and the readiness to be wholly fitted for God's use in the service of men. And here is still another who is ready to work as well as wait, but is looking for some great inflow of the Spirit's power to enable him to do mighty works, while he forgets that as a believer he already has the Spirit of Christ dwelling in Him, that more grace is given only to those who are faithful in the little, and that it is only in working that we can be taught by the Spirit how to do the greater works. All such, and all Christians, need to learn that waiting has working for its object, that it is only in working that waiting can attain its full perfection and blessedness. It is as we elevate working for God to its true place, as the highest exercise of spiritual privilege and power, that the absolute need and the divine blessing of waiting on God can be fully known.

On the other hand, there are some, there are many, who work for God, but know little of what it is to wait on Him. They have been led to take up Christian work, under the impulse of natural or religious feeling, at the bidding of a pastor or a society, with but very little sense of what a holy thing it is to work for God. They do not know that *God's work can be done only in God's strength, by God Himself working in us*. They have never learned that, just as the Son of God could do nothing of Himself, but that the Father in Him did the work, as He lived in continual dependence before Him, so, and much more, the believer can do nothing but as God works in him. They do not understand that His power can rest on us only as in utter weakness we depend upon Him. And so they have no conception of a continual waiting on God as being one of the first and essential conditions of successful work. And Christ's Church and the world are sufferers today, oh, so terribly, not only because so many of its members are not working for God, but because so much working for God is done without waiting on God.

Among the members of the body of Christ there is a great diversity of gifts and operations. Some, who are confined to their homes by reason of sickness or other duties, may have more time for waiting on God than opportunity of direct working for Him. Others, who are overpressed by work, find it very difficult to find time and quiet for waiting on Him. These may mutually supply each other's lack. Let those who have time for waiting on God definitely link themselves to some who are working. Let those who are working as definitely claim the aid of those to whom the special ministry of waiting on God has been entrusted. So will the unity and the health of the body be maintained. So will those who wait know that the outcome will be power for work, and those who work, that their only strength is the grace obtained by waiting. So will God work for His Church that waits on Him.

Let us pray that as we proceed in these meditations on working for God, the Holy Spirit may show us how sacred and how urgent our calling is to work, how absolute our dependence is upon God's strength to work in us, how sure it is that those who wait on Him shall renew their strength, and how we shall find waiting on God and working for God to be indeed inseparably one.

Believers are placed in the world with this one object, that they may let their light shine in good works so as to win men to God. As truly as the light of the sun is meant to lighten the world, the good works of God's children are meant to be the light of those who know and love not God.

Good Works,
the Light of the World

*Ye are the light of the world. Let your light shine before men,
that they may see your good works, and glorify your Father
which is in heaven.*

MATTHEW 5: 14, 16.

A LIGHT is always meant for the use of those who are in darkness, that by it they may see. The sun lights up the darkness of this world. A lamp is hung in a room to give it light. The Church of Christ is the light of men. The God of this world hath blinded their eyes; Christ's disciples are to shine into their darkness and give them light. As the rays of light stream forth from the sun and scatter that light all about, so the good works of believers are the light that streams out from them to conquer the surrounding darkness, with its ignorance of God and estrangement from Him.

What a high and holy place is thus given to our good works. What power is attributed to them. How much depends upon them. They are not only the light and health and joy of our own life, but in every deed the means of bringing lost souls out of darkness into God's marvelous light. They are even more. They not only bless men, but they glorify God, in leading men to know Him as the Author of the grace seen in His children. We propose studying the teaching of Scripture in regard to good works, and especially all work done directly for God and His kingdom. Let us listen to what these words of the Master have to teach us.

The aim of good works. It is that God may be glorified. You remember that our Lord said to the Father: "I have glorified thee on the earth, I have finished the work which thou gavest me

211

to do." We read more than once of His miracles, that the people glorified God. It was because what He had wrought was manifestly by a Divine power. It is when our good works thus too are something more than the ordinary virtues of refined men, and bear the impress of God upon them, that men will glorify God. They must be the good works of which the Sermon on the Mount is the embodiment—a life of God's children, doing more than others, seeking to be perfect as their Father in heaven is perfect. This glorifying of God by men may not mean conversion, but it is a preparation for it when an impression favorable to God has been made. The works prepare the way for the words, and are an evidence to the reality of the Divine truth that is taught, while without them the world is powerless.

The whole world was made for the glory of God. Christ came to redeem us from sin and bring us back to serve and glorify Him. Believers are placed in the world with this one object, that they may let their light shine in good works so as to win men to God. As truly as the light of the sun is meant to lighten the world, the good works of God's children are meant to be the light of those who know and love not God. What need that we form a right conception of what good works are, as bearing the mark of something heavenly and divine, and having a power to compel the admission that God is in them!

The power of good works. Of Christ it is written: "In him was life, and the life was the light of men." The Divine life gave out a Divine light. Of His disciples Christ said: "If any man follow me, he shall not walk in darkness, but have the *light of life.*" Christ is our life and light. When it is said to us, Let your light shine, the deepest meaning is, let Christ, who dwells in you, shine. As in the power of His life you do your good works, your light shines out to all who see you. And because Christ in you is your light, your works, however humble and feeble they be, can carry with them a power of Divine conviction. The measure of the Divine power which works them in you will be the measure of the power working in those who see them. Give way, O child of God, to the Life and Light of Christ dwelling in you, and men will see in your good works that for which they will glorify your Father which is in heaven.

The urgent need of good works in believers. As needful as that the sun shines every day, yea, more so, is it that every believer lets his light shine before men. For this we have been created anew in Christ, to hold forth the Word of Life, as lights in the world. Christ needs you urgently, my brother, to let His light shine through you. Perishing men around you need your light if they are to find their way to God. God needs you to let His glory be seen through you. As wholly as a lamp is given up to lighting a room, every believer ought to give himself up to be the light of a dark world.

Let us undertake the study of what working for God is, and what good works are part of this, with the desire to follow Christ fully, and so to have the light of life shining into our hearts and lives, and from us on all around.

Money . . . may be one of your choicest means of grace, a continuous fellowship with God in the renewal of your surrender of your all to Him, and proof of the earnestness of your heart to walk before Him in self-denial, and faith, and love.

Christ's
Estimate of Money

*Jesus beheld how the people cast money into the treasury: and
many that were rich cast in much. And a certain poor widow
came, and cast in a farthing. Jesus called his disciples, and saith
unto them, This poor widow hath cast more in than all: for all
they did cast in of their abundance; but she of her want did cast
in all that she had, even all her living.*

MARK 12: 41-44.

IN ALL our religion and our Bible study, it is of the greatest consequence to find out what the mind of Christ is, to think as He
thought, and to feel just as He felt. There is not a question that
concerns us, not a single matter that ever comes before us, but
we find in the words of Christ something for our guidance and
help. We want today to get at the mind of Christ about money;
to know exactly what He thought, and then to think and act just
as He would do. This is not an easy thing. We are so under the
influence of the world around us that the fear of becoming
utterly unpractical if we thought and acted just like Christ easily
comes upon us. Let us not be afraid; if we really desire to find
out what is His mind, He will guide us to what He wants us to
think and do. Only be honest in the thought: I want to have
Christ teach me how to possess and how to use my money.

Look at Him for a moment sitting here over against the
treasury, watching the people putting in their gifts. Thinking
about money in the church, looking after the collection, we often
connect that with Judas, or some hard-worked deacon, or the
treasurer or collector of some society. But see here—Jesus sits
and watches the collection. And as He does, He weighs each gift

215

in the balance of God, and puts its value on it. In heaven He does this still. Not a gift for any part of God's work, great or small, but He notices it, and puts its value on it for the blessing, if any, that it is to bring in time or eternity. And He is willing, even here on earth in the waiting heart, to let us know what He thinks of our giving. Giving money is a part of our religious life, is watched over by Christ, and must be regulated by His word. Let us try to discover what the Scriptures have to teach us.

1. *Money giving a sure test of character.* In the world money is the standard of value. It is difficult to express all that money means. It is the symbol of labor and enterprise and cleverness. It is often the token of God's blessing on diligent effort. It is the equivalent of all that it can procure of the service of mind or body, of property or comfort or luxury, of influence and power. No wonder that the world loves it, seeks it above everything, and often worships it. No wonder that it is the standard of value, not only for material things, but for man himself, and that a man is too often valued according to his money.

It is, however, not only thus in the kingdom of this world, but in the kingdom of heaven too, that a man is judged by his money, and yet on a different principle. The world asks, *What* does a man own? Christ, *How* does he use it? The world thinks more about the money getting, Christ about the money giving. And when a man gives, the world still asks, *What* does he give? Christ asks, how does he give? The world looks at the money and its amount, Christ at the man and his motive. See this in the story of the poor widow. Many that were rich cast in *much,* but it was out of their abundance; there was no real sacrifice in it; their life was as full and comfortable as ever, it cost them nothing. There was no special love or devotion to God in it; it was part of an easy and traditional religion. The widow cast in *a farthing.* Out of her want she cast in all that she had, even all her living. She gave all to God without reserve, without holding back anything; she gave all.

How different our standard and Christ's. We ask how much

a man *gives*. Christ asks how much he *keeps*. We look at the gift. Christ asks whether the gift was a sacrifice. The widow kept nothing over, she gave all; the gift won Christ's heart and approval, for it was in the spirit of His own self-sacrifice, who, being rich, became poor for our sakes. They—out of their abundance—cast in much: she—out of her want—all that she had.

But if our Lord wanted us to do as she did, why did He not leave a clear command? How gladly then would we do it. Ah, there you have it! You want a command to make you do it: that would just be the spirit of the world in the church looking at *what* we give, at our giving all. And that is just what Christ does not wish and will not have. He wants the generous love that does it unbidden. He wants every gift to be a gift warm and bright with love, a true free-will offering. If you want the Master's approval as the poor widow had it, remember one thing: you must put all at His feet, hold all at His disposal. And that, as the spontaneous expression of a love that, like Mary's, cannot help giving, just because it loves.

All my money giving—what a test of character! Lord Jesus! Oh, give me grace to love Thee intently, that I may know how to give.

2. *Money giving a great means of grace.* Christ called His disciples to come and listen while He talked to them about the giving He saw there. It was to guide their giving and ours. Our giving, if we listen to Christ with the real desire to learn, will have more influence on our growth in grace than we know.

The spirit of the world, "the lust of the flesh, the lust of the eye, and the pride of life." Money is the great means the world has for gratifying its desires. Christ has said of His people, "They are not of the world, as I am not of the world." They are to show in their disposal of money that they act on unworldly principle, that the spirit of heaven teaches them how to use it. And what does that spirit suggest? Use it for spiritual purposes, for what will last for eternity, for what is pleasing to God. "They that are Christ's have crucified the flesh and its lusts." One of the ways of manifesting and maintaining the crucifixion of the flesh is never to use money to gratify it. And the way to conquer every temptation to do so is to have the heart filled with large thoughts of the spiritual power of money. If you would learn to keep the flesh crucified, refuse to spend a penny on its gratification. As much as money spent on self may nourish and strengthen and comfort self, so money sacrificed to God may help the soul in the victory that overcometh the world and the flesh.

Our whole life of faith may be strengthened by the way we deal with money. Many men have to be engaged continually in making money—by nature the heart is dragged down and bound to earth in dealing with what is the very life of the world. It is faith that can give a continual victory over temptation. Every thought of the danger of money, every effort to resist it, every loving gift to God, helps our life of faith. We look at things in the very light of God. We judge of them as out of eternity, and the money passing through our hands and devoted to God may be a daily education in faith and heavenly-mindedness.

Very especially may our money giving strengthen our life of love. Every grace needs to be exercised if it is to grow; most of all is this true of love. And—did we but know it—how our money might develop and strengthen our love as it calls us to the careful and sympathizing consideration of the needs of those around us. Every call for money, and every response we give, might be the stirring of a new love and the aid to a fuller surrender to its blessed claims.

Money giving may be one of your choicest means of grace, a continuous fellowship with God in the renewal of your surrender of your all to Him, and proof of the earnestness of your heart to walk before Him in self-denial, and faith, and love.

3. *Money giving a wonderful power for God*. What a wonderful religion Christianity is. It takes money, the very embodiment of the power of sense of this world, with its self-interest, its covetousness, and its pride, and it changes money into an instrument for God's service and glory.

Think of the poor. What help and happiness are brought to tens of thousands of helpless ones by the timely gift of a little money from the hand of love. God has allowed the difference of rich and poor for this very purpose—that just as in the interchange of buying and selling mutual dependence upon each other is maintained among men, so in the giving and receiving of charity there should be abundant scope for the blessedness of doing and receiving good. Christ said, "It is more blessed to give than to receive." What a Godlike privilege and blessedness to have the power of relieving the needy and making glad the heart of the poor by gold or silver! What a blessed religion that makes the money we give away a source of greater pleasure than that which we spend on ourselves! The latter is mostly spent on what is temporal and carnal; that spent in the work of love has eternal value, and brings double happiness to ourselves and others.

Think of the Church and its work in this world, of missions at home and abroad, and of the thousand agencies for winning men from sin to God and holiness. Is it indeed true that the coin of this world, by being cast into God's treasury in the right spirit, can receive the stamp of the mint of heaven, and be accepted in exchange for heavenly blessings? It is true. The gifts of faith and love go not only into the Church's treasury, but into God's own treasury, and are paid out again in heavenly goods. And that not according to the earthly standard of value, where the question always is, How much? but according to the standard of heaven, where men's judgments of much and little, great and small are all unknown.

Christ has immortalized a poor widow's farthing. With His approval it shines through the ages brighter than the brightest gold. It has been a blessing to tens of thousands in the lesson it has taught. It tells you that your farthing, if it be your all, your gift, if it be honestly given (as you all ought to give to the Lord), has His approval, His stamp, His eternal blessing.

If we did but take more time in quiet thoughtfulness for the Holy Spirit to show us our Lord Jesus in charge of the Heavenly

Mint, stamping every true gift, and then using it for the Kingdom, surely our money would begin to shine with a new luster. And we should begin to say, The less I can spend on myself, and the more on my Lord, the richer I am. And we shall see how, as the widow was richer in her gift and her grace than the many rich, so he is richest who truly gives all he can.

4. *Money giving a continual help on the ladder to heaven.* You know how often our Lord Jesus spake of this in His parables. In that of the unjust steward He said, "Make friends of the mammon of unrighteousness, that they may receive you in the eternal habitations." In the parable of the talents He said, "Thou oughtest to have put *my money* to the exchangers." The man who had not used his talent, lost all. In the parable of the sheep and the goats, it is they who have cared for the needy and the wretched in His name, who shall hear the word, "Come, ye blessed of my Father."

We cannot purchase heaven—as little with money as with works. But in your money giving, heavenly-mindedness and love to Christ, and love to men, and devotion to God's work, are cultivated and proved. The "Come, ye blessed of my Father, inherit the kingdom," will take count of the money truly spent on Christ and His work. Our money giving must prepare us for heaven.

Oh, how many there are who if heaven and holiness could be bought for a thousand pounds would give it! No money can buy those. But if they only knew, money can wondrously help on the path of holiness and heaven. Money given in the spirit of self-sacrifice, and love, and faith in Him who has paid all, brings a rich and eternal reward. Day by day give as God blesses and as He asks—it will help to bring heaven nearer to you, it will help to bring *you* nearer to heaven.

The Christ who sat over against the treasury is my Christ. He watches my gifts. What is given in the spirit of wholehearted devotion and love He accepts. He teaches His disciples to judge as He judges. He will teach me how to give—how much, how lovingly, how truthfully.

Money—this is what I want to learn from Him above all—money, the cause of so much temptation and sin, and sorrow and eternal loss; money, as it is received and administered and distributed at the feet of Jesus, the Lord of the Treasury, becomes one of God's choicest channels of grace to myself and to others. In this, too, we are more than conquerors through Him who loved us.

Lord, give Thy Church, in her poverty—give us all—the spirit of the poor widow.

It is so easy to sin, even in giving . . .

The Holy Spirit
and Money

WHEN the Holy Spirit came down at Pentecost to dwell in men, He assumed the charge and control of their whole life. They were to be or do nothing that was not under His inspiration and leading. In everything they were to move and live and have their being "in the Spirit," to be wholly spiritual men. Hence it followed as a necessity that their possessions and property, that their money and its appropriations were subjected to His rule too, and that their income and expenditure were animated by new and hitherto unknown principles. In the opening chapters of the Acts we find more than one proof of the all-embracing claim of the Holy Spirit to guide and judge in the disposal of money. If I want as a Christian to know how to give, let me learn here what the teaching of the Holy Spirit is as regards the place money is to have in my Christian life and in that of the Church.

First we have: *The Holy Spirit taking possession of the money*. "All that believed were together, and had all things common; and they sold their possessions and goods, and parted them to all according as every man had need" (Acts 2: 44, 45). And again, Acts 4: 34: "As many as were possessors of land or houses, sold them, and brought the prices of the things that were sold, and laid them at the apostles' feet. And Barnabas, having a field, sold it, and brought the money and laid it at the apostles' feet." Without any command or instruction, in the joy of the Holy Spirit, the joy of the love which He had shed abroad in their heart, the joy of the heavenly treasures that now made them rich, they spontaneously parted with their possessions and placed them at the disposal of the Lord and His servants.

223

It would have been strange had it been otherwise, and a terrible loss to the Church. Money is the great symbol of the power of happiness of this world, one of its chief idols, drawing men away from God; a never-ceasing temptation to worldliness, to which the Christian is daily exposed. It would not have been a full salvation that did not provide complete deliverance from the power of money. The story of Pentecost assures us that when the Holy Spirit comes in His fullness into the heart, then earthly possessions lose their place in it, and money is valued only as a means of proving our love and doing service to our Lord and our fellow men. The fire from heaven that finds a man upon the altar and consumes the sacrifice, finds his money too, and makes it all *altar gold,* holy to the Lord.

We learn here the true secret of Christian giving, the secret, in fact, of all true Christian living—the joy of the Holy Ghost. How much of our giving, then, has there been in which this element has been too much lacking? Habit, example, human argument and motive, the thought of duty, or the feeling of the need around us, have had more to do with our charities than the power and love of the Spirit. It is not that what has just been mentioned is not needful. The Holy Spirit makes use of all these elements of our nature in stirring us to give. There is a great need for inculcating principles and fixed habits in regard to giving. But what we need to realize is that all this is but the human side, and cannot suffice if we are to give in such measure and spirit as to make every gift a sweet-smelling sacrifice to God and a blessing to our own souls. The secret of true giving is the joy of the Holy Ghost.

The complaint in the Church as to the terrible need of more money for God's work, as to the terrible disproportion between what God's people spend on themselves and devote to their God, is universal. The pleading cry of many of God's servants who labor for the poor and the lost is often heart-piercing. Let us take to heart the solemn lesson: this is simply a proof of the limited measure in which the power of the Holy Spirit is known among believers. Let us for ourselves pray most fervently that our whole life may be so lived in the joy of the Holy Spirit, a life so absolutely yielded to Him and His rule, that all our giving may be a spiritual sacrifice, through Jesus Christ.

Our second Pentecostal lesson on money we find in Acts 3: 6: "Then Peter said, Silver and gold have I none, but what I have that give I thee. In the name of Jesus Christ of Nazareth, walk!" Here it is: *The Holy Spirit dispensing with money.*

Our first lesson was: The Church of Pentecost needs money for its work; the Spirit of Pentecost provides money; money may be at once a sure proof of the Spirit's mighty working, and a blessed means of opening the way for His fuller action.

But there is a danger ever near. Men begin to think that money is the great need, that abundance of money coming in is a proof of the Spirit's presence, that money must be strength and blessing. Our second lesson dissipates these illusions, and teaches us how the power of the Spirit can be shown where there is no money. The Holy Spirit is the mighty power of God, now condescending to use the money of His saints, then again proving how divinely independent He is of it. The Church must yield herself to be guided into this double truth: the Holy Spirit claims all its money; the Holy Spirit's mightiest works may be wrought without it. The Church must never beg for money as if this were the secret of her strength.

See these Apostles, Peter and John, penniless in their earthly poverty, and yet by virtue of their poverty, mighty to dispense heavenly blessings. "Poor, yet making many rich." Where had they learned this? Peter says, "Silver and gold have I none; in the name of Jesus Christ, walk." It points us back to the poverty which Christ had enjoined upon them, and of which He had set them the wonderful example. By his holy poverty He would prove to men that a life of perfect trust in the Father is how the possession of heavenly riches makes one independent of earthly goods, how earthly poverty fits the better for holding and for dispensing eternal treasures. The inner circle of Christ's disciples found in following the footsteps of His poverty the fellowship of His power. The Apostle Paul was taught by the Holy Spirit the same lesson. To be ever in external things utterly loose even from earth's lawful things is a wonderful—he almost appears to say, an indispensable—help in witnessing to the absolute reality and sufficiency of the unseen heavenly riches.

We may be sure that as the Holy Spirit begins to work in power in His Church, there will again be seen His mighty operation in the possession of His people. Some will again by their giving make themselves poor in the living faith of the incomprehensible worth of their heavenly heritage, and in the fervent joy the Spirit gives them in it. And some who are poor and in great straits with their work for God will learn to cultivate more fully the joyful consciousness: "Silver and gold have I none; what I have I give: in the name of Jesus Christ, walk." And some who are not called to give all will yet give with an unknown liberality, because they begin to see the privilege of giving all, and long to come as near as they can. And we shall have a Church, giving willingly and abundantly, and yet not for a moment trusting in its money, but honoring those most who have the grace and the strength to be followers of Jesus Christ in His poverty.

Our third lesson is: *The Holy Spirit testing the money.* All the money that is given, even in a time when the Holy Spirit is moving mightily, is not given under His inspiration. But it is all given under His holy supervision, and He will, from time to time, to each heart that honestly yields to Him, reveal what there may be wanting or wrong. Listen: "Barnabas, having a field, sold it, and brought the money. *But* Ananias sold a possession and kept back part of the price, and brought a certain part, and laid it at the apostles' feet." Ananias brought his gift, and, with his wife, was smitten dead. What can have made the gift such a crime? He was a deceitful giver. He kept back part of the price. He professed to give all, and did not. He gave with half a heart and unwillingly, and yet would have the credit of having given all. In the Pentecostal Church the Holy Ghost was the author of the giving: Ananias' sin was against the Holy Ghost. No wonder that it is twice written, "Great fear came upon the whole church, and upon all who heard it." If it is so easy to sin even in giving, if the Holy Spirit watches and judges all our giving, we may well beware and fear.

And what was the sin? Simply this: Ananias did not give all he professed. This sin, not in its greatest form, but in its spirit and more subtle manifestations, is far more common than we think. Are there not many who say they have given their all to God, and yet prove false in the use of their money? Are there not many who say all their money is their Lord's, and that they hold it as His stewards, to dispose of it as He directs, and yet who, in the amount they spend on God's work, as compared with that on themselves, and in accumulating for the future, prove that stewardship is but another name for ownership.

Without being exactly guilty of the sin of Judas, or Caiaphas, or Pilate in crucifying our Lord, a believer may yet partake with them in the spirit in which he acts. Even so we may be grieving the Holy Ghost, even while we condemn the sin of Ananias, by giving way to the spirit in which he acted and withholding from God what we have professed to give Him. Nothing can save us from this danger but the holy fear of ourselves, the very full and honest surrender of all our opinions and arguments about how much we may possess, and how much we may give, to the testing and searching of the Holy Spirit. Our giving must be in the light, if it is to be in the joy of the Holy Ghost.

And what was it that led Ananias to this sin? Most probably the example of Barnabas, the wish not to be outdone by another. Alas, how much there is of asking what men will expect from us! The thought of the judgment of men is present to us more than the judgment of God. And we forget that our gifts are accounted of God only by what the heart gives: it is the wholehearted giver that meets Him. How much the Church has done to foster the worldly spirit that values gifts by what they are in men's sight, in forgetfulness of what they are to Him that searches the heart!

May the Holy Spirit teach us to make every gift part and parcel of a life of entire consecration to God. This cannot be till we be filled with the Spirit: this can be, for God will fill us with His Spirit.

4. There is still a lesson, no less needful, no less solemn than that of Ananias (Acts 8: 18-20): *The Holy Ghost rejecting money.*

"Simon offered them money, saying, Give me also this power. . . . But Peter said to him, Thy money perish with thee, because thou hast thought to obtain the gift of God with money." The attempt to gain power or influence in the Church of God by money brings perdition.

Here, more than with Ananias, it was simple ignorance of the spiritual and unworldly character of the Kingdom of Christ. How little Simon understood the men he dealt with. They needed money, they could well use it for themselves and for others. But the Holy Spirit, with the powers and treasures of the unseen world, had taken such possession of them, and so filled them, that money was as nothing. Let it perish rather than have anything to say in God's Church. Let it perish rather than for one moment encourage the thought that the rich man can acquire a place or a power which a poor man can not acquire.

Has the Church been faithful to this truth in her solemn protest against the claims of wealth? Alas for the answer its history gives! There have been noble instances of true apostolic succession in the maintenance of the superiority of the gift of God to every earthly consideration. But too often the rich have had an honor and an influence given them, apart from grace or godliness, which have surely grieved the Spirit and injured the Church.

The personal application is here again the matter of chief importance. Our nature has been so brought under the power of the spirit of this world, our fleshly mind, with its dispositions and habits of thought and feeling, is so subtle in its influence, that nothing can deliver us from the mighty spell that money exacts but a very full and abiding enjoyment of the Spirit's presence and working. To be entirely dead to all worldly ways of thinking, the Holy Spirit alone can give us. And He can give it only as He fills us with the very presence and power of the life of God.

Let us pray that we may have such a faith in the transcendent glory, in the absolute claim and sufficiency of the Holy Spirit as God's gift to the Church to be her strength and riches, that money may be ever kept under Christ's feet and under ours, that we may recognize its only worth to be for His heavenly ministry.

God has nothing for us but Jesus. Anything beyond that God cannot give us . . .

God Is Love

He that dwelleth in love dwelleth in God, and God in him.
1 JOHN 4: 16.

How LITTLE we know what we are! To think that that Everlasting God who created heaven and earth should deal with each one of us individually—with *me*—and that it should please Him to fill me with that everlasting love in which He begot the Son and in which the Holy Spirit maintains the fellowship between Father and Son!

"God is love." You find these words twice in the fourth chapter of the first Epistle of John. "God is love." What does that mean? I think it means, at once and first of all, that I seek just not for love, for I may fail. If I want love I must seek God, for love is the very nature of God. It does not say God *has* love, but God *is* love, and the love that I need is God Himself coming into my heart. Not a drop of pure, real, heavenly, everlasting love can come to us but that God must be moved to give it as an act of His grace. God has revealed His love in all nature, even in the very animals. Look at the way the little lamb clings to its mother and the way the mother sheep cares for the lamb. That is what we call love. And so amongst the most savage and most ungodly heathen you can find love of a certain sort. But the love of heaven, the love of eternity, that will last; the love that is not in the flesh, but that comes from heaven—that love is God, and if I want that love I must have God. What a thought! Oh, let the heart bow in humble praise! I want this great God to come unto me and to take possession of me and to make me a vessel fit for His use, that He can fill me with love. Let the heart say: "Yea,

231

my God, take me and fill me with love, for the sake of Thy Son who died on Calvary."

The first question is, "What do we need, what is it we seek?" Then our second question will be, "What are we to do, what have we to do to get what we are seeking?" And then the third question, "What are we to expect?"

Look, first of all, at your relationship to God! Do you know the love of God as you ought to know it? Does it dwell on you as an overshadowing power, the way the love of a mother dwells on the child that lives in her smile?

Do you know the love of God, and does it make you, from morning to night, sing the song of the ransomed ones? There is not a heart but says: "Oh, I know the love of God too little." And why is that? It is because you have not been perfected in love, because when the soul is perfected in love it has such a sense of that love that it can rest in love for eternity, and though it has as much as it can contain for the time being, it can always receive more. Again, is there no dissatisfaction with your love to God? You sometimes think that you can say, "Oh, my God, I do love Thee." There are many Christians who don't say that—real Christians. They are afraid to say it. They fear God, and they say earnestly, "I wish to love God," and they complain very honestly and bitterly, "Oh, my God, why have I so little love?" But they hardly know what it is to say, "Oh, thou God of Heaven, how I love Thee! Thou knowest how my heart delights in Thee." Have you not had to confess often and often that you could not speak like that to God? And does there not come up in the heart a strong feeling of condemnation, "Alas, my love to God is not what it should be"? And then sometimes when you have a sense of God's love given to you for a moment in your fellowship with God, is there not a cry, "Oh, why can it not abide with me?" The child has no trouble in rejoicing in its parents' love. I remember my little boy or girl of five or six, sometimes coming to the study door, and opening it, and just looking in and smiling to see papa's face, and then shutting the door and going away happy; or coming on tiptoe just outside the window, looking in to see papa, and then going off again to play. It was never an effort to the child to love the father. Dear friend, God can do that for you, and make it so that His love shall all the day cover you, and that your love shall all the day rise up to Him in deep restfulness and in childlike peace. I am sure God can do it. This is what we need— more love, more love, more of the love of God.

And then look further. What is it we need? Look at our love to those around us, in our daily life, in our family, husband and wife, parents and children, brothers and sisters, masters and servants.

Look at our daily life in business! Look at our daily life in society, with the people whom we meet. Remember the remarks about others that are so easily made. Think of the hasty judgments, of the sharp words, of the thoughtless expressions that escape our lips. Think of how many there are on whom our eyes look and there is no outgoing of love toward them. And why is it such an effort to us, and why do we come short? I want you to get hold of one thought, and that is that love is the easiest and most natural thing in the world—if I have it in me to love—the easiest and happiest thing in the world, if I only have it in me. But if I do not have it, then I try and try to do it for a little and then I fail. Is not God able? I believe He is, and you believe it too. Is not God able to take such possession of the heart of His child? Is not God able, in His mighty power as God, to come into the heart of His child and to give His love and His spirit? Is not God able to open a fountain of love, so that in all our intercourse day by day it shall be Love, Love, Love flowing out unceasingly? Christ said: "Hereby shall all men know that ye are my disciples, if ye love one another." But, oh, the Church of Christ has become a proverb for its contentions and divisions! How terrible! And within the circle of the same little church, of the same little society, of the same little mission, oh, how often between Christians distrust and jealousy, how often unlovingness and harshness! Oh, do you not feel in your own home and in your own circle and in your business that there is just one thing needed? If my heart was filled with God's love, how easy it would be to live to His glory!

And then there is one thing more. I must not only think of my relation to God and my relation to my fellow men around me, but I must especially think of my work.

What is it that is wanted in the work of the Church, and why is there so much complaint of want of power and want of success? The one thing that is wanted is the infinite love of God dwelling in us. What would that do for us? It would give us more than one thing. In the first place, it would give us a wonderful tenderness and gentleness and meekness and humility in dealing with people. What is one of the chief marks of Christ Jesus that makes Him so pleasing to the Father? It is His humility. "Learn of me, for I am meek and lowly in heart." He made His way to the throne of glory in meekness and humility.

Tell me, is not that what is needed in our work—that the spirit of tender compassion and of gentleness breathing in every utterance about the people whose souls we are seeking should be the mark of Christ's presence? And then more love would not only make us gentle, but, as with Christ Himself, it would also be the power and the inspiration of a divine zeal, so that we would sacrifice all. If we loved others with the love of God, how much more power there would be in our work, how much more sacrifice of time and of ease in praying to God for souls, how much more intercession! Oh, if we loved aright, how much more sacrifice of comfort, how often would we work as I read of a couple of missionaries in China some years ago, asking, "What more can we sacrifice for Jesus?"

If the love of God possessed us, how we would sacrifice everything for souls—our formality, our routine, our habits, the ways we have learned to walk—how they would pass away! Not only would we do more work, but different work—work breathed upon by the love of God. And then, when we have the divine fire, the divine fire of Christ, the Lamb of God, the Spirit of the Lamb, who gave Himself to the cross, when that is in us, something passes unconsciously and unwittingly out of us on to the people; they do not know what it is, and we do not know; but how many unconverted men would be converted by the power of God's love! Is not this what every worker needs? It is the one thing the Church needs, and—bless God—it is the one thing He wants to give us.

Suppose we see truly our need in our relation to God and to society and to the work we have to do for Christ. "What have we to do?" The first thing is, there will have to be the discovery and confession of sin. We must not only confess our need, but we must go far deeper. Take the word "perfect love" as a light or lamp from Heaven and flash it, first of all, into our own hearts and lives and look at our lives in the light of that perfect love. Turn the light of that word "perfect love" on Christ, to find out what there is in Him and what He is able to do. Find out exactly what Christ can give us, what Christ can do for us, and how we can become possessed of the life and the love shown in Him for us. Then take this flashlight that we have turned upon ourselves first and then upon the face of Jesus, and turn it upon the face of the world, upon the work we have to do in our own immediate circles and in heathendom, and then in the light of the word of perfect love go afresh to work for Jesus.

We must begin with ourselves, to let the light shine upon ourselves and upon our life. And what does that mean? It means that there will have to be within us a distinct discovery of where we fail. I am not going to make out a list of transgressions against the law of love. But suppose we have made the discovery of how far we have come short in thought and word and deed of this life of perfect love. What then? Are we to come with these sins to God? Yes, and yet that is not enough. What we need is this, to find out what is the root of all. And what is that? Here I have been a Christian for ten or twenty or thirty years, praying for God to give me love. What is it that is like a devil within me, so that I cannot love? What is this temper or this evil spirit? What is this coldness of disposition? God will lead us to see what is at the root of all. And what is it? Just one word—Self, Self, Self!

When God created Adam he gave him self-life; with what object? That Adam should bring that self-life to God to be filled with God's life. And Adam turned away from God and had that self-life closed against God. That is the corruption you and I have inherited from Adam—self. If grace comes into a Christian and begins to work in his heart and the seed of life is planted amidst the mass of surrounding corruption, how the Christian strives and fights and prays and wrestles to conquer, but in vain! It is self that is the one, only cause of his failure. It tries to pluck off a fruit here and a bud there; it cuts off one branch after another of this terrible foe to love. It vows and strives and perhaps does grow a little in love, yet at the bottom does not have rest, and why? There is that something there that will not love. Oh, may God discover to us that terrible something! Self! Self! Self! We shall then understand that nothing less than death, the death to self, is what must come, if the love of God is to live in us. Thus to come to God, in the confession that there is that in us which must die, and which we cannot slay, is the first step we have to take.

The next thing will be a fresh surrender to God. But, oh, I think that with many it must be a different surrender from what they have hitherto made! You know many people honestly surrender themselves to God, but never understood what it is to surrender self. There is a great difference between surrendering yourself and surrendering your self as we use the word "self," giving up your whole self as you are, that root out of which all the evil comes. Many a man says, "Oh, yes, I want to give myself up to God, just as I am, that He may save me," and yet has never understood what the self is that has to be given up, and what the meaning is of giving it up to God. But God teaches the upright; He teaches him through deep humiliation, and then a man finds out, "I did indeed turn to God, and yet I never turned away from myself. I took myself with my old will and temper, as I was, and gave myself to God; but that was not what God wanted. God wanted me to turn away from self." That is the surrender we must ask God to teach us—to give up this accursed self. Dear friends, do you want to realize perfect love to God in this world? Does that self-will hinder? You must find out some way of dealing with that self, and you cannot deal with it yourself. It is only the love of God coming in that will cast out self; and before God will do that, self must be brought like a criminal, must be laid at His feet.

There is no cure for self but death. We must die to self. How can I do that? I cannot kill myself; I cannot be my own executioner. I cannot nail myself to the cross. God alone is the death of self. God Himself must do it. He allowed Christ to die on the Cross, and then when Christ had died God raised Him up. That is why, when God brings a man to see all that there is in Christ and to receive Christ fully, the power of Christ's death can come upon him and he can die to sin; and if he dies to sin he dies to self. How can a man be dead to sin if he is not dead to self? Self is the very root of sin. There is no sin if there is no self. You can take away men's sins, and you can adorn the inner man until you think there is no sin there; but if self is there, sin also is there. Let us ask God that He may teach us what it is to have self given up. Let us, then, ask God for grace to give up ourselves to Him as we have never done before. Friends, God is love.

Will you let Him come in? Will you surrender yourself to God? There is another thing that surrender to God implies. When you have come and surrendered yourself, you must now keep your place as one actually given into God's hands, in deep resignation, looking to Him for what He will do. Wait upon Him to quicken you and to make you alive from the dead. These are the three things we shall need—confession, surrender, and faith. That faith means this: faith in the power of God, who raised Christ from the dead. Yes, the resurrection of Christ is the law of the new life.

Christ Jesus was born in Bethlehem, and just so I am born

again by the Holy Spirit. But Christ Jesus had to be born again the second time. He had to live and be tried, tempted and tested, to be developed and to be perfected, and then He had to give up His life, and out of the grave, when He was in hopeless, helpless, dark death, God raised Him up. That is what the Christian must come to. The birth in Bethlehem is the likeness of my new birth when I was converted, but the birth from the grave when Christ became the first-born of the dead is the likeness and promise of that full birth, in which the power of the death and life of Christ come into me, and I know what it is to be dead with Christ and risen with Him—dead unto self and made alive unto God. Let the one great thing that you do from the morning early when you awake, to the evening when you go to sleep, be this, "Have trust in God" for what He can do in making you partakers of Christ's death as the death to self, and His life as a life to God and in God, a life in perfect love. Say to God: "My Father, I trust in Thee for what Thou alone canst do," and say to yourself, "I am going to believe in God, in the mighty power with which He raised Christ from the dead to work in me and in God's children around me."

"What are we to expect?" We know what we are seeking and we know what we have got to do, but now comes the question, "What are we to expect?" My answer is, "Let us expect something beyond all expectation." We have so often limited God by our thoughts, and we are doing it still. Yet Paul speaks of "love that passeth knowledge," and then says further, "God is able to do above all that we can ask or think." Now prepare yourself for something that passeth knowledge, for something that is above what you can think, and give God the honor of doing something divine. Then, further, if you ask, "What must I expect?" I would sum it up in these words: "Jesus Himself." The work of God the Father is to beget God the Son, and that is the work which goes on through eternity. When we read of the eternal generation, that does not mean that it was a thing in the past. Eternity —what is eternity? Eternity is ever going on. It is an ever-present now, and the one work of God the Father is to beget the Son. What do I expect? I expect God to give to all who are prepared the indwelling Christ in their hearts, in a power they have never known, so that they may get rooted and grounded in love, and know the love that passeth knowledge. That is what we need and what we may expect. God has nothing for us but Jesus. Anything beyond that God cannot give us, but God is willing and able to give this—the living Son born afresh into us. And then He reveals Him to us, and when the living Christ dwells in us, He will break open the fountain of love within us. That is what we want. Expect it now. Fix your eye upon Jesus, Jesus Himself. He must do it. He has done it. He has taught us on Calvary what it is that He gave up His life for, that in His fellowship with us our old man might be crucified with Him. He has done it all for us. We want God to reveal to us what that means, and to make us partakers of it. You may say: "I have so often tried to believe in Jesus, but there has been so much failure and I am so ignorant." Paul prayed that God would strengthen believers mightily by the Holy Spirit. It is only the Father who can reveal the Son, and He does it only by the Holy Spirit.

When Jesus dwells in us, then we are filled with love unto all the fullness of God—the Triune God, not only in Heaven, but in our hearts. Fix your hearts upon this: the Father must do it, and what the Father will do, I must expect—the Father, God Almighty, to give this Jesus into my heart as an indwelling Saviour; what the Father does is to strengthen us with might by the Holy Spirit in the inner man. Expect that. Fix your heart upon God. That is the one way to the Father, and as you go along, step by step, let your heart be filled with this: God is Love. Love is the Divine omnipotence. Love is the life and the glory of God. Yes, God is Love. There is the love of the Father, and the love of the Son, and the love of the Spirit. Let us fix our hope in the love of the Father giving the Son into our hearts. Let us rejoice in the Son coming with God's perfect love to dwell within. Let us bow in stillness while the Holy Spirit works mightily within us to shed abroad the love. God will come unto us, and will bring us into His banqueting house, and His banner over us will be love. May God teach the waiting heart to expect this, nothing less than the Perfect Love of God perfected in us.

God's children must acknowledge each other wherever they meet, however they may differ in their church organizations or in other things. My brother must be as dear to me as Jesus Christ is. God's children must draw close together, or the gift of perfect love cannot come.

Our Lord's Prayer

Father, that the love wherewith thou hast loved me may be in them.

JOHN 17: 26.

IF I WANT to find out the nature of perfect love I must look up to God's love to Christ. The text says: "Father, that the love wherewith thou hast loved me may be in them." This is Christ's conclusion of His whole prayer. It is the whole object of His work, and that object is this: That the love that I have tasted, that the love which rested on me, and dwells in me, may now pass on to them. And so, if you want to know what the life of perfect love is, you must rise up to heaven itself and see what the love of God to Christ is.

And if you ask: How can I know what this perfect love in the Godhead is? I can answer only, The Father gave His own life to the Son; the Son was begotten of the Father, out of His bosom; in the depths of the Godhead Christ came forth from the Father. If God had not been love, if God had been anything that we could call selfish, He would have been content to be God alone. But He would not be alone. From eternity He set His Son before Him as His image and His glory. He gave birth to the Son. When a man gives out his own life to another, that is love; and the love of God is that He gave all His life to His only begotten Son, and He said that, to all eternity, He never would live without His Son.

Here I learn the first lesson, that love means this—a birth out of the heart of God. That is the only true love upon earth. Love that will live and last through eternity. Even now it can come only out of the Godhead. It is the work of God to give that birth;

243

and, dear friends, as really as Jesus Christ was born of God, and in the resurrection was perfected as the first begotten from the dead, you must be born of God in the power of the resurrection, or you have no share in the love of God or in the heaven of God. Let us remember this. If we try to learn the lesson, I think God will teach us more and more that love means giving, and giving all. We sometimes give a little, but not all. To give all—that is love! What did the Father do to the Son? He made Him heir of all things. The Father let Christ share in everything. God gave Him a seat on His Throne; He gave Him a place in the worship of the angels; by Him he created the world; He gave Him all His glory and all His love.

Do you want to know what love is? Oh, my heart cannot take it in, nor my tongue express it; my thoughts cannot reach to all its fullness. Love means—giving all! It is that with God, and it is that with us too. If you are to have love, it means you are to give up everything to God, everything. God cannot be limited. With God, love means giving His life to His Son and with that giving everything! That is the love of God to Christ.

How did God prove His love for Christ? He gave Him His own life, He gave Him all things throughout the universe, and then sent Him to die! You say, That is strange; is that the love of God? Yes. Oh, you say, that was an exceptional thing, which became necessary, but did not belong to the essence of God's love. No, indeed; this sending His Son to die is the highest and most wondrous part of God's love to Christ. And how does it prove the love of God? I will tell you. It was not possible in the nature of things that God should come to die upon earth for sinners, but God put the honor on His Son when He said: "Go and become a man, and in love live the life of man and of humanity." It was the infinite love of the Father to the Son which made Him say, I will put this honor on my Son. God in His love sent Christ to die. We have heard that, in different ways, love always means death, the death of self; and God sent Christ and said: "Go and obey my word, and then lay down thy life to die to sin and the world and self; give up thy life entirely for me and my glory."

My friend, as you think of the love of God, has it ever said to you that you must die? The highest point of God's love is that He invites us to die utterly to self, to be like Himself and His Son, perfect in love. God's love to Christ means death. May we have grace to say: I would enter into the death of Jesus, I would be nothing in myself, O my God! May Thy love consent to accept of me to be nothing.

And then God raised Him from the dead: that also was the love of God, which led Christ in the path of death to the resurrection life, the resurrection glory, the eternal glory of heaven. If you want to learn the nature of love, remember these three things —that love gave birth to the Son, that love gave all to the Son; and then love claimed all from the Son. Oh, if we are to know perfect love, do not let us think this is too high for simple people. Do not let us say we cannot be troubled with theological doctrines about the relation of the Father to the Son. If we are to spend eternity with God, in the fellowship with the Father and the Son, there is surely nothing of such absorbing interest for us as to know what the relation of the Father and Son is. God gave His Son to me and with Him gave all; and now love is—God claiming everything. Only as I die can I enter into the new, the resurrection life, into perfect love, into the glory of God.

There is a second thought in this passage. I must look not only at the love of the Father to Christ, but I also must look at the love of Christ to us.

How do I get that from this text? Very simply. Jesus prays, "Father, that the love wherewith thou hast loved me may be in them." What does that imply? Christ wants to share the love God gave to Him with us, and He goes to the Father and says, "Father, here are those whom I have redeemed. Father, I plead that they may have all the love that thou hast given me, and that it may rest in them." Is not that Christ's wonderful love? The Father took Christ up into a perfect likeness with Himself. As He had given all to the Son in the depth of Godhead, He allowed the Son to show on earth what love is by giving back all to the Father. And Christ wants us to grow up into a perfect likeness with Himself. As God gave all He had to Christ, so Christ gives all He has to us, even to the love of the Father. It is the love of Christ that prays to the Father that the Father's love may come into us. What does that teach us? It reminds us of what Christ is doing in Heaven. Christ as a mighty King on the throne of God prays day and night for us. He gives up his life in glory to pray for us. He cannot die a second time, but just as He died on the Cross on earth, He gives up His life in Heaven to prayer that the love of God may come down upon us. Oh, friends, that is what love does. You tell me you want to know what love will do.

Love will pray for others. It will say, just like Christ, "I have this wonderful blessing of God's love, and I will give it to those around me. It should be our prayer, "Oh, let the love of God come down upon them also!" There is nothing that should make Christians so ashamed as their non-appreciation of the influence of intercession for others. How many Christians who have thought everything was right with them; who spend their little time in prayer daily, their quarter-hour or half-hour and get benefit from it, and yet have never made it a rule to make time for prayer for others! Have you ever set your heart on the thought, "I can by much prayer bring down a blessing from heaven on someone else"? Love calls on God. It comes to God as the fountain of love, and has something to say. It gives its time and its ardent heart's desire and says, "Father, oh for a blessing on those around me." Jesus the King spends all His time in heaven praying. Do you believe it? It is true. And how much time do you spend in this loving exercise? How little of this love we have! Father, forgive us. If you want to know what love is, look at the love of Christ praying for us.

And, then, just think further of what Jesus said in the rest of that prayer, of how He spoke of what He had done for those disciples: "I have given them thy word," and in the words that precede our text He says, "I have declared thy name unto them." Love not only prays; Love works.

Christ had been working for three years on those disciples. How patiently He had borne with them. How marvelously He had instructed them and led them step by step, humbling Himself to their weak capacities! Love not only prays, but it teaches, it watches and it labors. Remember, if we study this perfect love in the light of Christ's love, it means that we give up ourselves to pray for others and to work for others.

And then one thing more. Christ not only prays and works, but He dies. He says in this chapter, "I sanctify myself; I give myself as a sacrifice for them that they may be sanctified."

Love dies for those it loves. You remember those solemn words in I John: "If Christ died for us, we ought to lay down our lives for the brethren." There ought to be such love in us that we give our lives for the brethren that, when it becomes needful, dying for them would be the natural result of our love. Love not only prays; love labors. Love not only labors; love dies. God's love is seen in that He gave Christ up to the death as an honor and a privilege. Christ's love was seen in that He gave His life. Perfect love gives its life for others. It is true in God, in Christ, in ourselves.

The third thought to which this text leads us is the conditions on which this perfect love can be ours. For whom does Christ pray in this prayer? "That the love wherewith thou hast loved me may be *in them*, and *I in them.*" Is that for the whole world? No. For whom, then? He gave certain marks of those for whom He asked that God's love should be in them. These marks indicate the conditions that are required if we are to receive this blessing of the perfect love of God in our hearts. What are these marks? The first is this— "They are not of the world as I am not of the world." Separation out of the midst of the world. Oh, Christians, if you want to know what perfect love is, you must come out of the world; you must be separate. You tell me, "I do not understand what that means." Never mind. Say to

God, "Lord, I want to come out of the world; I want to live like a man who is not of this world but of the other world." The love of God cannot dwell in your heart if the spirit of the earth is there. It is impossible. It is only when we go out from the world that the love of God can enter into and take possession.

Another mark. Christ says, "I have given them Thy Word, and they have received it and they have believed that Thou hast sent me." That is another mark—receiving the Word in obedience and faith. They forsook all to follow Christ, and they received His word and testimony, set their whole confidence on it, and that is what St. John sets before us as the mark of perfect love. "Whoso keepeth his word, in him verily is the love of God perfected." Let me say this for your comfort: the love and the faith of these disciples for whom Christ prayed was very defective, and yet Christ accepted it as the obedience and the faith of loving hearts. And so we can be sure that if we come to Christ with our feeble beginnings He will receive our love, and, day by day, will lead us in the path of perfect love and perfect obedience— not the obedience of angels, but the perfect obedience of faith. That is the second condition of love. The first condition is separation from the world; the second, obedience to His Word; and the third is unity with believers around us. Christ prays for that: "Father, that they may be one." God's children must acknowledge each other wherever they meet, however they may differ in their church organizations or in other things. My brother must be as dear to me as Christ Jesus is. God's children must draw close together, or the gift of perfect love cannot come. In the fellowship of love they must prove to the world that there is something in them that is different from the world, that the Spirit of God and Heaven, of Perfect Love, is in them. Dr. Saphir has said somewhere that in the Primitive Church there were many differences, but that so long as they looked more on the things on which they agreed than those on which they differed, the unity of love would be maintained unbroken.

If the Church of Christ had only done that, how different

would be our state today! But we have been looking too much on the things on which we differ, though many of these things are comparatively of little importance. Do let us get hold of the thought that, just as we must be separate from the world, and joined to Christ in obedience to His Word, so also we must be joined to each other.

My love to my brother is the sure, the only real, test of my love to God and to Jesus. If we are to seek and to find the life of Perfect Love, if God's love to Christ is to be in us, as He prays, and He in us, the condition must be fulfilled—we must give up ourselves to see that all our intercourse with God's children is love—unselfish, tender, self-sacrificing, ministering love.

But lest any be discouraged by the fear that these conditions of the path to perfect love are beyond their reach, let me remind them of one thing.

In Holy Scripture we find a great deal about two stages in the Christian life—the Old Testament and the New, a time of preparation and a time of fulfillment. The longer I study God's word and the Christian life, the deeper grows my conviction that the difference between the Old Testament and the New Testament is a radical one, and runs not only through the life of the Church, but through the life of every believer.

Now, it is for His disciples Christ is praying as He asks, "Father, that the love wherewith thou hast loved me may be in them, and I in them." It would seem this was something that had not yet come. They did indeed love Jesus, but their love was an elementary, a feeble love, the love of beginners. Christ had said, "If ye love me, keep my commandments." No doubt they went away from that sacred hour with full purpose to keep His word, and yet how soon they forsook their Master! Christ saw that they did indeed love Him and longed to obey Him; He Himself said, "The spirit is willing, but the flesh is weak." Christ saw their loving obedience, but they were still only in the preparatory stage, and their best efforts were but feeble. "To will, is present with me, but how to perform that which is good, I find not": this was their experience. And yet they were in the sure path to perfect love. Christ was training them for something better: amid all their failure He saw their heart was right with Him. Thank God for the comfort that can give us.

There is another stage: it is this that Christ prays for. He seems to say, "Father, there is a new time coming, when Thou shalt pour down Thy Holy Spirit upon them; when the love of God shall fill them as it fills me; when Thy love in which I live shall be in them as in me, and I in them." Christ was praying for the Day of Pentecost; the three conditions without which the Day of Pentecost could not come were found in them. And the Day of Pentecost came, and God's love filled them. Our heart may be saying honestly: "Perfect love, yes, perfect love. This is my constant plea," and yet we feel we have not attained to it. Let us hold on in the spirit to these three things—separation from the world, from its spirit, and from its pleasures; acceptance of God's Word in faith and obedience; unity with all God's children; and Christ who led His disciples on so wonderfully will lead us on too.

We now come to the fourth thought that this text suggests. The love of God perfected in us.

This is what Christ prays for: "Father, that the love wherewith thou hast loved me may be in them, and I in them." This refers to the Day of Pentecost. In John 14: 20 Christ says, *"At that day* ye shall know that I am in my Father and I in you." He also said, "If ye love me, keep my commandments, and the Father will love you." There was a love to Christ which was already in them. There was also a love which they were still to get through the Holy Spirit. This they obtained at Pentecost, and this we must have if we would know perfect love. And the question comes to us, "What does it mean to have the love of the Father in us, the love wherewith the Father loved His Son? What does God aim to accomplish in us? "That the love wherewith thou hast loved me may be in them"! First of all, I must understand that the love of God is going to be within me. How is the love of

God, possessing and ruling and filling my inmost being, to be in me? Just as thinking and feeling and willing are in me, and it is most easy and natural for me to think and feel and will. Even so, when the love of God really fills my heart, love will flow out spontaneously and continuously. Instead of it being a duty, as it is in the earlier disciple stage, with its effort and failure, it becomes a delight, and there is a love that cannot help loving, because God's love has been shed abroad and has taken complete possession. Up to this time there has been an inward life of self continually getting the mastery. The love of self and of sin has been very deep in me. What Christ's prayer asks and promises is, that we are now to have an inward life of love; in the place of sin and self the love of God to Christ is now to fill the heart. Instead of having to try to love always, and so often failing, love comes in as an indwelling Divine power, constituting the very life of the soul, and loves spontaneously, continuously, and most joyfully. Love has filled the heart. Think of this. My heart, *My* heart, MY heart becomes the habitation of the holy love of God to Jesus in its Divine joy and blessedness, its infinite power, its everlasting glory! "That the love wherewith thou hast loved me may be in them"! That love is to be *in us,* our second nature, our new self, our very selves.

And, then, note further, this love is to come through the Holy Spirit. Yes, the work of the Holy Spirit is this: that in and through Him the Father begets the Son. He is the love which is their living bond of union. You know it is a doctrine of the Church that the Spirit proceeds from the Father and the Son; and therefore, when Christ met the Father in the glory after His resurrection, the Holy Spirit began to flow; and the Father gave the Spirit to the Son and the Spirit flowed down from the Father through the Son to the disciples. And it is to this Holy Spirit we are now to look to bring the love of God as a heavenly reality, as a Divine life, into our hearts. We have the Holy Spirit. So the disciples had the Holy Spirit also before the Day of Pentecost, but only as a secret power working in them. They did not know

Him as a Person. They had Him given to live within them, but they did not know Him. They could not, indeed, yet know Him as bringing the very love of Christ to them from the throne of God in the glory. And just so there are the two stages in our experience.

We may struggle and wrestle, and try to fight for love, but we don't succeed. But the words of our text give us the precious promise which gives us hope. As the Son prays to the Father, "That the love wherewith thou hast loved me may be in them," so we receive the blessed assurance that through the power of the Holy Ghost our hearts can be filled with the love of God in a way and to an extent that we have never known before.

Once more. If you want to know how this love of God is to be perfected, it is not only that you have to give the whole heart and wait for the Holy Spirit of God; but, above all things, you have to look to Jesus, through whom the Spirit comes and whom the Spirit will reveal. See how Christ connects the two things. "That thy love may be *in them, and I in them.*" The indwelling love of God and the indwelling Son of God are inseparable.

You cannot understand it, but the Son of God is the love of God. He was born of God's love; He was sent by God's love; He was raised from the dead by God's love; and He dwells in the glory of God's love. And, therefore, while we look for the Holy Spirit, let us set our hearts wide open, and know that we can have within a holy temple that can be filled with love, because Christ, who holds within Himself all God's love, comes to dwell there. Let us expect this with a trust and a confidence and a clinging to Christ, "In whom the love of God is manifested." And as the prayer of Jesus brought Pentecost to the early disciples, so the prayer of Jesus brings Pentecost to the individual soul now. It is the intercession of Christ which can bring Pentecost and perfect the love of God in our hearts.

Let me ask two simple questions. Do *you* believe that this prayer can be fulfilled in *you?* Do you believe that it is God's will that the Holy Spirit should reveal his love to Jesus as a living reality and a continuous experience within your heart? I believe it! I believe it is God's will for you and for me. Perfect love is the love that is in God, that is in Christ, that is in the Holy Spirit for us, that He may bring it into our hearts. The fruit of the Spirit is love. Oh, look at the mystery of the love of the Father to Christ His Son, the love that fills eternity. Look at the love of the Son to us, heavenly love made manifest on earth. The love that the Spirit brings is this very same Divine and heavenly love, and this perfect, Divine love, the Holy Spirit will pour out in our hearts. Let us fix our faith on this. There is a perfect love for me, and the Holy Spirit is the messenger to come and bring it through Jesus and from Jesus to me. Nothing short of this can satisfy the longing soul, and I want it in my heart; I may count upon it. Why? Because Jesus prayed the Father that it should come. Have you set your heart upon that, and do you believe God means that it can come? The love wherewith the Father loved the Son is a Divine supernatural reality, a heavenly power, to dwell in and have possession of you.

Come, listen for a moment to the voice of Christ: "Father, thou lovest me, and I love them; according to the riches of thy glory grant that the love wherewith thou hast loved me may enter the hearts of my disciples, and dwell there always, so that I can dwell there." Let us say, "Father, I believe it can be done!"

And then my second question: If you believe it can be done are you going to yield yourself to it? Love claims all. Love is very exacting. God asked Christ to give His life up to Him, and He could not do anything else, and Christ asks of His disciples that they should forsake all for Him; Christ asks that we should be ready to give up our life for the brethren. Perfect love wants a perfect heart, perfectly given up to love alone. It asks that we should yield ourselves and say, "Lord, here I am, and I part with everything in the world that love may have possession of every word I speak and every thought I have and every act I do, that every moment of my life may be a sacrifice to Thy love, so that nothing but love can come out of me!" Are you afraid to speak thus? Do you feel as if you did not dare to pray thus, because you know not how it can come? It must come as a Divine supernatural gift, as the power of God. It is not a thing which can be attained, or reached, or grasped. But are you willing to surrender yourself to be like Christ, nothing but a servant of Divine love? It is a very solemn thing that our love for God on the Day of Judgment is going to be tried by our love for man and our treatment of our fellow man. We have to be judged by the test of love. Do remember that. You are not going to get into heaven by faith without works, but by faith and works of love. You get pardon by faith without one good work, but in the Day of Judgment good deeds are to be taken into account. Remember that every day as you come to God He judges of your love to Him by your conduct to your fellow men. What do we read in John? "Let us not love in word, but in deed and in truth, and we shall assure our hearts before God." "He that loveth not his brother whom he hath seen, how can he love God whom he hath not seen?" Your love for God is an imagination, a sentiment, a delusion, if your heart is not full of love for your fellow man.

Oh, this perfect love comes as a very solemn claim, with its demand on every moment of my life that the world around may see that it is real. Are you willing to give up your life to it? Are you willing to submit to God, that the love with which God loved Christ, the love that sent Him to die for men, may have you wholly for itself? God wants us to say, "My God, I give myself up to live only, and always, and wholly for the love of God." You feel it is impossible, you feel utterly helpless; you cannot undertake to live this life of perfect love. Fear not, the more helpless, the better.

We need to sink right down into despair. It was after Christ was dead!—dead!—dead and in the grave, that God raised Him up to the glory; and you must sink down into death and utter helplessness and say, "My God, I want love, and my love is passing away from me; oh, be Thou my support!" You must sink down into the grave of your own impotence, the grave of self, and let God Himself lift you up! If only you are willing to acknowledge God's claim and say, "My Father, here I am. This love, wherewith Thou didst love Thy Son, it is too high for me —beyond my reach. But if Thou wilt hear His prayer, here I am; let that love enter and take possession. I yield myself to its blessed power—let it live in me!"

Will you claim this? Will you accept this? I know it is not an easy thing.

Perhaps, you think that you are not now prepared for it; but come, come now. Do you really believe there is such a thing as the words of this prayer being fulfilled in your spirit? Is it possible?

Can you say your "Yea and Amen, O my God"? And then are you willing to surrender absolutely your whole life, day by day to wait upon God for the power and love of God to maintain within you the life of perfect love, of God's love to Christ living in you?" And then the last question. Are you ready now in faith to believe in the mighty power of the Holy Spirit to bring the full answer to the prayer, "That the love wherewith thou hast loved me may be in them, and I in them"? Are you ready to believe that God will grant what is written in His Word, "love perfected in us; we perfected in love"? God holds out the promise. The mighty, all-prevailing intercession of Christ pleads for it. The Holy Spirit can and will work it. The Three-in-One God is my surety for it. Lord, I do believe; grant it for Thy Name's sake. Amen.